U0901190

《中央民族大学民族博物馆馆藏文物集粹》

编委会

中央民族大学民族博物馆馆藏文物集粹

滇藏遗珍

茶马古道上的马帮文物

马晓华 编

薛林 任奎艳 译

Relics from Yunnan and Tibet
Caravans' Artifacts on the
Ancient Tea-Horse Road

辽宁民族出版社
·沈阳·

图书在版编目（CIP）数据

滇藏遗珍：茶马古道上的马帮文物：汉英对照 / 马晓华编；薛林，任奎艳译．— 沈阳：辽宁民族出版社，2023.6
（中央民族大学民族博物馆馆藏文物集粹）
ISBN 978-7-5497-2826-8

Ⅰ．①滇… Ⅱ．①马… ②薛… ③任… Ⅲ．①马—商业运输—历史文物—中国—图集 Ⅳ．① K870.2

中国国家版本馆 CIP 数据核字（2023）第 017976 号

滇藏遗珍：茶马古道上的马帮文物
DIAN-ZANG YIZHEN: CHA-MA GUDAO SHANG DE MABANG WENWU

出版发行者：辽宁民族出版社
地　　址：沈阳市和平区十一纬路 25 号　邮编：110003
印 刷 者：辽宁新华印务有限公司
幅面尺寸：210mm × 285mm
印　　张：18.25
字　　数：150 千字
出版时间：2023 年 6 月第 1 版
印刷时间：2023 年 6 月第 1 次印刷
责任编辑：尹　瑛　王　智
封面设计：杜　江
责任校对：王　荷

标准书号：ISBN 978-7-5497-2826-8
定　　价：300.00 元

网　　址：www.lnmzcbs.com　　邮购热线：024-23284335
淘 宝 网 店：http://lnmz2013.taobao.com
如有印装质量问题，请与出版社联系调换　　联系电话：024-23284340

总　　序

我国是一个统一的多民族国家，各民族在悠久的历史长河中创造了辉煌璀璨的中华文化，构建了休戚与共的中华民族命运共同体。各民族在长期的生产实践中，创造的众多具有历史、艺术、科学、文化价值的民族文物，是中华民族文明成果的重要组成部分。少数民族文物作为中华文化的重要承载者与中华民族命运共同体的重要物证，记录了各民族在不同时期的社会制度以及生产生活的历史轨迹，具有不可再生性和不可替代性。保护和研究民族文物，对了解我国各民族灿烂文化和悠久历史，促进民族团结和社会主义精神文明建设，铸牢中华民族共同体意识，具有重要意义。

中央民族大学民族博物馆始建于1951年，是以全国少数民族及民族地区文物为主要收藏、展示和研究对象的专业博物馆。作为我国建馆时间最早、规模最大、藏品最多的民族类专业博物馆之一，建馆七十余年来，一直秉承服务社会、服务教学科研的宗旨，在收藏、展示、研究等方面注重专业积累，至今已经成为具有一定规模和丰富民族文化内涵的民族类专业博物馆。

中央民族大学民族博物馆现藏有民族服饰、民间文书、宗教器物、马帮文物以及民族乐器、民族酒器、生产工具、生活用具、古器物等十余类文物，共5万余件（套）。藏品具有如下特点：一是族属、内容丰富，全国56个民族的各类文物几乎均有收藏；二是以各民族民间传统服饰、首饰居多，这些服饰充分反映了各民族人民在纺织、印染、刺绣、鞣制皮革等方面的卓越才能和精湛技艺；三是民间文献，特别是云南地区清代、民国契约文书数量，在全国首屈一指；四是许多藏品都具有重大的政治和历史纪念意义，如中华人民共和国成立初期各族人民献给中央政府的大量珍贵礼品；五是不乏具有很高历史与艺术价值的珍品，如新旧石器时代的石器，商周时期的青铜器，秦汉以来的铜镜、铜鼓、陶俑、瓷器、古钱币、字画，元、明、清时期的古扇，蒙古、藏等民族贵族阶层使用的金银器皿，藏族的唐卡，黎族的龙被，畲族的祖谱图，藏传佛教和伊斯兰教的珍贵宗教器具和典籍，藏、傣、彝、纳西、水等民族的古籍等；六是台湾少数民族文物数量大、时代早、精品多。

中央民族大学民族博物馆藏品主要来源有清华大学原社会学系多年收集的各类民族、民俗文物；有原中央民族访问团到各民族地区收集的民族文物；有各民族同胞敬献给中央政府的各类物品；有原江苏省文管会移交来的旧国立边疆教育文化馆的各类文物；有民族学家杨成志、吴泽霖、林耀华、吴丰培、胡先晋、宋蜀华等教授从各民族地区收集来的民族文物；还有民族地区一些单位的赠送及移交的民族文物；有 20 世纪 80 年代以来征集的人口较少的民族文物；还有近几年新征集的大量的西南民族地区民间文物等。丰富的馆藏为民族文化传承和研究提供了珍贵的历史文化资料和艺术资料，为学科建设服务奠定了基础。

近几年来，学校领导高度重视民族博物馆的建设，不断加大资金、设备和人才投入力度。全馆设备已更换一新，藏品库房已实现恒温恒湿，馆藏文物的数字化建设已经奠定基础，文物的补充征集和研究工作也在同步进行。从 2013 年开始，按照国家文物局和国家民委的新藏品登记标准，我们已基本完成馆藏品建档建账、入库归位工作。上述工作为文物的保护、管理、研究以及数据库建设打下坚实基础。

民族博物馆以铸牢中华民族共同体意识为主线，为巩固和发展“中华民族一家亲，同心共筑中国梦”理念，承担起了宣传民族政策、普及民族知识、展示民族艺术、弘扬民族文化的责任。中央民族大学民族博物馆作为全国民族团结进步教育基地、北京市校外教育基地、北京市海淀区爱国主义教育基地，是民族文化知识普及传播的重要基地。

中央民族大学民族博物馆为了宣传和展示民族文物收藏、保护工作成就，弘扬各民族优秀文化，促进与博物馆各界的交流合作，与辽宁民族出版社共同推出了《中央民族大学民族博物馆馆藏文物集粹》系列丛书，包括乐器卷、背孩带卷、马帮文物卷、古扇卷、服饰卷等。

中央民族大学民族博物馆将与时俱进，逐步建设和发展成为一个研究型、开放型和民族特色鲜明的高水平民族学博物馆，并为提高教学和科研服务质量而不懈努力。

中央民族大学民族博物馆馆长　张铭心

2023 年 3 月 31 日

General Preface

China is a multi-ethnic unified nation, whose various ethnic groups have created glorious Chinese civilization and formed the community for the Chinese nation in which to share weal and woe. The peoples, over the course of history, have made a lot of culturally-valuable artifacts constituting an integral part of Chinese civilization. The non-renewable and irreplaceable artifacts from the ethnic minorities, as the bearer of Chinese culture and the physical evidence of the community for the Chinese nation, record their social systems and historical traces of their life and production in different periods. Preservation and study of the ethnic artifacts is significant in gaining insight into the brilliant Chinese cultures and long history, promoting ethnic unity and socialist cultural and ethical progress, and forging a strong sense of community for the Chinese nation.

Founded in 1951, the Museum of Ethnic Cultures, Minzu University of China is devoted to collection, display and study of cultural relics from the ethnic minorities and ethnic areas in China. As one of the earliest and largest museums with richest collection, it has, over 70 years, been committed to serving the community, teachers and researchers, focusing on professional development in collection, exhibition and study, hence becoming a sizable specialized museum with a rich collection of ethnic cultural objects.

The Museum of Ethnic Cultures, Minzu University of China is home to 50,000 pieces (sets) of cultural objects, falling into about 10 categories, such as ethnic costumes, non-governmental documents, religious objects, caravans' artifacts, musical instruments, drinking vessels, production tools, implements for daily life, ancient utensils. They are summed up as follows: A. the museum collection varies greatly in kind and covers almost every ethnic group in China; B. ethnic costumes and jewelry constitute the majority, showing the ethnic groups' remarkable talent and super craftsmanship in spinning and weaving, printing and dyeing, embroidery, leather tanning, etc.; C. non-governmental documents, especially contractual ones in Yunnan during the Qing dynasty and the Republic of China, rank top in quantity across China; D. many of them are politically and historically significant, for example, the numerous gifts to the central government from all the ethnic groups in China in the early period of PRC; E. some of them have high value of history and art, for example, stone-wares in Paleolithic and Neolithic periods, bronze vessels in the Shang and Zhou dynasties, bronze mirrors, bronze drums, terracotta figurines, porcelains, ancient currency, painting and calligraphy since the Qin and Han dynasties, ancient fans in the Yuan, Ming and Qing dynasties, gold and silver utensils used by Mongolian and Tibetan aristocrats, Tibetan Thang-ga, the Li people's tapestries with auspicious ornaments, the She people's family tree, precious religious objects and scriptures in Tibetan Buddhism and Islamism, and ancient books of Tibetan, Dai, Yi, Naxi and Shui peoples; F. the objects from Taiwan ethnic groups are relatively numerous, early, and exquisite.

The collection of the Museum of Ethnic Cultures, Minzu University of China has largely come from the following sources: ethnic and folk relics acquired by the former department of sociology, Tsinghua University; those acquired by the former Central Visiting Missions when visiting ethnic regions; those to the central government from various ethnic groups; those in the collection of the Republican State-run Educational and Cultural Center for Border Areas and handed over by the former Jiangsu Commission of Cultural Heritage Administration; those collected by such ethnologists as Prof. Yang Chengzhi, Prof. Wu Zelin, Prof. Lin Yaohua, Prof. Wu Fengpei, Prof. Hu Xianjin and Prof. Song Shuhua in various ethnic areas; those presented as gifts or handed over by the organizations in some ethnic areas; those collected from the less populous ethnic groups since the 1980s; and those acquired in recent years from private collections in the southwest ethnic areas. The rich collection provides culturally, historically and artistically valuable information for studying and carrying forward ethnic cultures and lays a solid foundation for helping with the construction or development of relevant subjects in the school.

In recent years, the school leadership has emphasized the development of the museum, increasingly founding and investing in upgrading equipment and attracting more senior professionals. The museum is now state-of-art, temperature and humidity being kept constant, and the digitization of the collection well begun while research and efforts in collecting supplementary relics also under way. Beginning in 2013, in accordance with NCHA and NEAC's new standard for registration of cultural objects, the documentation of the collection is almost finished and a clear location for each piece in the storeroom is made. The aforementioned pays the way for preservation, management and study of cultural objects and for the construction of database.

With the sense of community for the Chinese nation being raised as top priority and “The Chinese nation is a close family, building the Chinese dream together.” as a principle, the museum is committed to publicizing the ethnic policy, popularizing ethnic knowledge, displaying ethnic arts, and carrying forward ethnic cultures. As the national base for education on ethnic unity and progress, the Beijing base for after-school education, and Beijing Haidian District base for patriotic education, the museum has become a major venue for popularizing and spreading ethnic cultures.

The museum, together with Liaoning Ethnic Publishing House, has launched “Masterpieces from the Collections of the Museum of Ethnic Cultures at the Minzu University of China” series, including books for Musical Instruments, Baby Carriers, Caravans' Artifacts, Ancient Fans, Costumes, in order to publicize and display cultural relics in the collection and achievements in preservation, carry forward ethnic cultures and promote cooperation between the museum and other organizations.

The Museum of Ethnic Cultures, Minzu University of China will keep pace with the times and become a first-class research-based and open-type museum with typical of ethnic cultures, and make a sustained effort to serve the teachers and researchers better.

Zhang Mingxin
Director of the Museum of Ethnic Cultures, Minzu University of China
March 31, 2023

前　言

茶马古道是形成于秦汉，兴于唐宋，盛于明清的交通、贸易与文化交流通道。它主要穿行于今藏、川、滇横断山脉地区和金沙江、澜沧江、怒江三江流域，是从云南、四川等茶叶产区以马（包括骡、牛、牦牛等）驮、人背为主要运输方式，把内地的茶及日用品等运往青藏高原，又将青藏高原地区所产的马、骡、毛皮、药材等物品输入内地进行交换，同时伴随丰富的跨地域、跨民族社会文化交流的古道网络和连接纽带。茶马古道是中国西南各民族自古以来交往、交流、交融的走廊，推动了区域和民族文化的传播与交融，对中国统一的多民族国家的形成、发展和维护具有重要的历史作用。20 世纪 70 年代以后，由于公路、铁路和空中航运等现代交通基础设施的不断建设和开通运营，以及现代商贸的兴起，茶马古道才渐渐淡出了历史舞台。

茶马古道连接了中国西部广阔的少数民族地区，其沿线是中国民族文化最富集的地区之一，是中国西南各族人民和睦共处、互惠互济、同生共荣的历史见证，也是边疆和内地各民族“谁也离不开谁”亲密关系的生动体现。茶马古道所经之地，居住着汉族、藏族、傣族、彝族、白族、纳西族、阿昌族、德昂族、景颇族、怒族等 20 多个民族。一千多年来，这条茶马古道如一条吉祥的红绳，将大西南边境多个民族的生活乃至精神世界联结到了一起。在这世界上地势最高、最险峻，地理形态最为复杂的传统商贸通道上，穿梭于崇山峻岭、丛林深处与苍茫雪原之间的马帮，是促进商贸和文化交流的重要媒介，他们歇息落脚于客栈、锅庄，或投宿于村寨，活跃在民间，无数次的来来往往，源源不断地将各种货物和文化养料传输到所经之地，开阔了人们的视野，丰富充实了人们对异域的想象，激发、带动了更多形式的区域和人民交往。在那里，不同的民族节日被共同欢庆，不同的民族饮食被彼此接纳，不同的民族习俗被理解尊重，多姿多彩的文化接触、碰撞、互补、融合，形成“你中有我，我中有你”的新文化形态，使青藏高原和横断山区成为多元一体文化的典型区域。

在茶马古道沿途可以见到许多十分相近的岩画和石棺墓葬；在藏羌民族的碉楼院房里，五音阶的丝竹旋律隐约有傣家凤尾竹的婆娑之声；在昌都，既有金碧辉煌的喇嘛寺，也有关帝庙、土地祠等汉文化的建筑。云南德钦的奔子栏因其特殊的地理位置，进出西藏的马帮都会在那里休整，从而

穿行在崇山峻岭中的马帮

拿着铜锣的赶马人和行走的马帮头骡

云南普洱茶马古道斑鸠坡路段

在野外宿营做饭的马帮

滇藏茶马古道云南大理凤阳邑

成为滇藏茶马古道上多民族文化的交汇之地。奔子栏的各民族一起过春节，除夕之夜，人们围着篝火，跳起弦子舞、锅庄舞。奔子栏的藏族妇女服饰明显有多民族融合的特征，即普米族式的大包头、蒙古族式的夹袄、彝族式的百褶裙；大小中甸的藏族服饰明显受到纳西族和白族的影响，在头帕、围腰、坎肩上都有所体现；宁蒗永宁的摩梭男人常年行走西藏，受藏族马帮影响深刻，至今穿的完全是藏装。文化的和谐促进了血缘的亲和，茶马古道促成了民族深度的交往和融合，不同民族联姻的家庭在这里大量产生，有的人家甚至有五个民族的成员生活在同一个屋檐下，民族团结之花盛开在茶马古道上。

茶马古道给我们带来各民族之间友谊的记忆，是彼此间互助互惠、唇齿相依、休戚与共的具体呈现，是各民族资源共享、分工协作的结果和对美好生活的追求。它成为不同民族文化圈之间的连接纽带与文化认同的催化剂，促进了区域间的民族交往、交流、交融，深化了国家认同，有力推动了中华民族共同体的形成与发展。

茶马古道以滇藏线、川藏线、青藏线、滇桂线为主线。我们今天所说较为成熟和定型的茶马古

依旧存活的茶马古道古集市——云南剑川沙溪寺登街

滇藏茶马古道上的阿墩子古城

滇藏茶马古道上的独克宗古城

道，基本是指明清时期确定和延续下来的川藏线和滇藏线。滇藏线主要是从西双版纳、普洱、临沧等产茶区经景东、凤庆、南涧、巍山、大理、剑川、鹤庆、丽江、香格里拉后，进入西藏的芒康，过昌都、林芝，最后到达拉萨。

自 2016 年以来，中央民族大学民族博物馆陆续从滇藏线茶马古道重镇巍山征集了近千件茶马古道的遗物，主要包括马帮交通、生活、护身用具，以及马店的牌匾、用品，交易的工艺品、药材，还有当地马锅头传家之物等。我们从中精选出 260 余件将其拍照编撰成册，旨在通过这些实物资料，重温那段珍贵的历史记忆，让我们仿佛还能听到马铃声声，感受赶马人的一路艰辛和马背上承载的沉甸甸的人生梦想。通过茶马古道遗物上许多中原文化美好寓意的吉祥图案和纹饰，蒙古族牧区的餐刀在茶马古道上被广泛地使用，以及藏族马帮护身挂件的一面是六字真言、另一面是八卦纹饰等细节，深刻理解茶马古道是一条多民族交往、交流、交融的河流，是内地与边疆，汉、藏及西南各民族通过交往、交流而逐渐聚合的历史见证，是民族团结的象征和纽带，因此也是最有意义的记忆载体和共享符号，对于铸牢中华民族共同体意识具有重要的作用和意义。

Preface

The Ancient Tea-Horse Road refers to a network of routes for transportation and the exchange of goods and ideas among different cultures, which appeared in the Qin and Han dynasties, became popular in the Tang and Song dynasties and peaked in the Ming and Qing dynasties. It winds across what is now called Hengduan Mountains and the reaches of Jinsha River, Lancang River and Nujiang River in Tibet, Sichuan and Yunnan, along which tea from Yunnan and Sichuan and necessities were carried by pack animals (horses, mules, oxen or yaks) and by humans on foot to Qinghai-Tibet Plateau and horses, mules, fur and leather and medicinal herbs to inland. Since ancient times, the Tea-Horse Road has been a corridor for the contact, interaction and blending between ethnic groups in southwest China, promoting the spread and exchange of regional and ethnic cultures and playing a historically significant role in the formation, development and safeguarding of China as a multi-ethnic, unified country. From the 1970s, the Road lapsed into disuse because of the construction and use of modern transport infrastructure like new roads, railroads and airports and the rise of modern trade and business.

The Ancient Tea-Horse Road linked the vast ethnic regions in southwest China, which is one of the areas where the most diverse cultures co-exist, historical evidence that all the peoples there co-existed in harmony, reciprocity and prosperity and demonstrates the close relation — "No one can separate from each other." — between the frontier and inland. Where it goes through is inhabited by over 20 peoples like Han, Tibetan, Dai, Yi, Bai, Naxi, Achang, De'ang, Jingpo, and Nu. For over 1,000 years, like a red auspicious thread, it linked the ethnic groups in the southwest frontier physically and spiritually. Along this traditional trading road with the highest altitude, the most precipitous terrain and most complex topography, across towering mountains, thick jungles and snow-covered areas travelled caravans, who were the key mediums for promoting the trade and cultural exchanges. They stayed in inns and Tibetan-style business brokers', or put up in hamlets and villages, interacting actively with local people so that their countless journeys kept bringing all kinds of goods and cultural ideas to where they passed, broadened the horizon of the locals, enriched the locals' imagination of other areas, stimulated more forms of interaction between peoples and regions. Out there, various ethnic festivals were observed; different ethnic foods were accepted; dissimilar ethnic customs were understood and respected; and diverse cultures interacted, conflicted, complemented, and blended, causing a new form of culture— "cross-fertilization", and making Qinghai-Tibet Plateau and Hengduan Mountains a typical area of pluralistic integration of cultures.

Along the Ancient Tea-Horse Road, a lot of similar rock paintings and stone coffins are seen; in Diaolou (Tibetan-style house), a pentatonic-scale melody by traditional stringed and bamboo wind instruments sounds somewhat like the Dai's flavor; in Changdu, splendid lamaseries, Temples of Guanyu and Earth Temples co-exist. In Benzilan, Deqin, Yunnan, because of its special location, caravans going into and out of Tibet would make a rest stop, so it became a meeting-point of multi-cultures. All the ethnic groups in Benzilan celebrate the Spring Festival and people dance Xianzi Dance and Guozhuang Dance around a fire on the Eve of Spring Festival. What Tibetan women wear there clearly suggests a mixture of many cultures, namely Pumi-style turban, Mongolian-style lined jacket, and Yi-style pleated skirt; in Zhongdian, Tibetan costumes obviously reflect influences from Naxi and Bai in turban, waist warmer and sleeveless jacket; Mosuo men in Yongning, Ninglang wear Tibetan costumes because they travel to Tibet all the time and are greatly influenced. Cultural blending makes mixed marriages possible, and the Road facilitates closer ethnic interaction and blending, numerous mixed marriages arise. Some families consist of members of five ethnic origins, a typical example of ethnic unity on the Road.

The Ancient Tea-Horse Road reminds us of the friendship between all the ethnic groups, which is a reflection of mutual help, interdependence, sharing weal and woe, a result of resource sharing and division of labor and a quest for better life. It has become the link between various ethnic cultures and a catalyst for cultural identity, promoting the contact, interaction and blending between ethnic regions, strengthening the national identity, and greatly driving the formation and development of the community for the Chinese nation.

The Ancient Tea-Horse Road consists mainly of Yunnan-Tibet route, Sichuan-Tibet route, Qinghai-Tibet route, and Yunnan-Guangxi route. The regularly travelled pathways we mention today chiefly refer to Sichuan-Tibet and Yunnan-Tibet routes that have existed since the Ming and Qing dynasties. Yunnan-Tibet route starts from Xishuangbanna, Pu'er and Lincang where tea is grown, through Jingdong, Fengqing, Nanjian, Weishan, Dali, Jianchuan, Heqing, Lijiang, Shangri-la, then into Mangkang in Tibet, through Changdu and Linzhi, finally to Lhasa.

Since 2016, the Museum of Ethnic Cultures, Minzu University of China has gradually collected about 1,000 relics related to the Road from Weishan, a hub on the Yunnan-Tibet route, including caravans' vehicle and devices, necessities, self-protection tools, and caravansaries' plaques, utensils, traded handicrafts and medicinal herbs, and leader of local caravan's relics. We have selected 260 pieces from the collection and have had them photographed and compiled into the book so as to relive those valuable moments in the past through physical materials, allow us to hear the jingle bell again, and experience the horse driver's hardship on the road and imagine their life dream on horseback. From the auspicious designs and patterns on the relics of the Road widely used in the central plains of China, from the much-used Mongolian knives on the Road, and from the Tibetan caravans' amulet pendant with the six-word mantra on one side and the Eight Trigrams on the other, we deeply understand the Ancient Tea-Horse Road as a river of multi-ethnic contact, interaction and blending, as historical evidence of inland and frontiers, and Han, Tibetan and various peoples in the southwest coming together gradually through contact and interaction, as a link and symbol of ethnic unity, and as a meaningful memory vehicle and shared sign, hence playing a significant role in forging a strong sense of community for the Chinese nation.

目录

目录

目录

第一单元　滇藏茶文化

Part I　Tea Culture in Yunnan and Tibet

茶虽然只是茶马古道中重要的商品之一，但它打破了地理的屏障、民族的界限以及不同政治与信仰带来的隔阂，融入了大部分民族和民众的血脉中，见证着人类千百年来基于物质生活而又脱离物质生活的精神追求，因此学者把它作为首字命名古道。最使人感到茶之力量的是这样一句藏族古谚语："加察热！加霞热！加梭热！"译为汉语就是："茶是血！茶是肉！茶是生命！"可见茶、马、古道成了连结不同民族文化的纽带。沿着茶马古道，茶从中国走向了世界，成为中国文化的象征之一。

Tea, as one of the important goods on the Ancient Tea-Horse Road, has overcome geographical handicap, broken down the ethnic barriers caused by different political opinions and religious beliefs and blended into the blood of most ethnic groups and people, witnessing the peoples' age-old spiritual quest based on material life but going beyond the reality, hence scholars has used it as the first word of the name for the Road. As the old Tibetan proverb goes, "Tea is blood, tea is flesh, tea is life." showing the potency of tea. So tea, horses and the road have become the bonds of various ethnic cultures. Along the Ancient Tea-Horse Road, tea has gone global, becoming a symbol of Chinese culture.

茶原产于以云、贵、川为主的中国西南地区，这是世界上最早发现、利用和栽培茶树的地方，也是茶马古道起始的地方。云南境内澜沧江流域的西双版纳、普洱、临沧等地，满目的常绿阔叶林，山高、湿热、雾大，有广阔的茶园，是茶树之乡。澜沧江沿岸的许多地名都和茶有关，傣语中“勐腊”意为“茶叶之乡”。今云南镇沅千家寨现存最早的茶树已有2700年历史。景谷发现的宽叶木兰化石是3540万年前的木兰科植物留下的历史斑痕，同时也是迄今唯一发现的茶树植物垂直演化的始祖，为引证茶树最原始产地提供了古植物依据。茶树之乡构成了天然的野生型、过渡型、栽培型品种齐全的世界茶树博物馆，谱写出人类发现、驯化、种植和利用茶的文明史。

关于澜沧江两岸茶叶种植的最早记载见于唐代樊绰的《蛮书》。书中记载1200多年前南诏时期的普洱景东、景谷及以南地区，世居在此的民族已经种植茶叶，他们有独特的烹茶和饮茶方法，在茶中放入椒、姜、桂烹而饮之。现今在云南普洱景迈山古茶园，世居民族创造性地采用“林下茶”的种植方式，形成“林茶共生，人茶共荣”的茶文化景观，且延续传承近千年，依旧生机勃勃。故景迈山古茶园在2012年就已进入中国“世界文化遗产”预备名单。2023年9月17日，在联合国教科文组织举办的第45届世界遗产大会上，中国“普洱景迈山古茶林文化景观”申遗项目顺利通过，成功列入《世界遗产名录》，成为全球首个以“茶”为主题的世界文化遗产项目。

中国名茶之一的普洱茶，其得名是因为清雍正七年（1729年）置普洱府，辖今普洱市、西双版纳及大部分临沧等产茶地区，并设“茶局”和“总茶店”，专办茶引（执照）、茶税及督办贡茶厂。普洱茶制作加工工艺独特，以云南所产的大叶种茶为原料，经萎凋、杀青、揉捻、晒干等工艺后制成晒青毛茶，晒青毛茶经蒸压制成生普洱，晒青毛茶再发酵后蒸压制成熟普洱。

据光绪《普洱府志》载，普洱茶早在唐代就已行销西域一带及西部边境地区。普洱茶一般有饼茶、沱茶、砖茶、金瓜茶等形制。藏族爱喝的酥油茶多用砖茶和沱茶来制成，茶中含有茶多酚、咖啡因、氨基酸、维生素等，就像青藏高原上流淌的生命之血，不仅可以解渴、消除油腻感，还能补充藏族因饮食结构单一而缺乏的各种维生素，因此深受藏族人民喜爱。在2022年暑期考察调研访谈时，奔子栏的藏族餐馆老板告诉我们，他们喝的酥油茶放盐，是咸的，而西藏的藏族喝的酥油茶放糖，是甜的，有利于缓解高原反应。

1659年清政府正式把普洱茶列入贡茶案册，并主要以马匹驮运进京，因连遭抢劫，从1839年开始不再进京。2005年“马帮茶道·瑞贡京城”普洱茶文化北京行活动，组织了120匹骡马，云南省11个民族的43位赶马人于同年5月1日从宁洱出发，历经云南、四川、陕西、山西、河北和北京五省一市，行程4000多公里，于10月中旬将5吨多茶叶驮载到北京，再现了300多年前普洱府奉命贡茶进京的历史盛事。云南马帮一路风餐露宿、历经艰辛，把马帮文化沿途一路传播，用沿途的善款为途经的省市各援建了一所希望小学，重走马帮路所收获的精神和成果值得人们欣赏和赞叹。

西双版纳贺开古茶园里的一号古茶树

云南镇沅千家寨世界野生茶树王

云南景迈山古茶林茶神树

云南澜沧芒景布朗族村寨茶祖树

Tea originated in southwest China, mainly in Yunnan, Guizhou and Sichuan, where tea was first discovered, used and grown, and was also the starting point of the Ancient Tea-Horse Road. Xishuangbanna, Pu'er and Lincang in the Lancang River basin of Yunnan are the hometown of tea, where there are evergreen broad-leaf forests everywhere and vast tea plantations with high mountains, humid climate and dense fog. The names of many places along the Lancang River are associated with tea, for example, "mengla" in the Dai language means the "hometown of tea". The oldest living tea tree is 2,700 years old in Qianjiazhai, Zhenyuan, Yunnan. The broad-leaf lily magnolia fossil found in Jinggu is the historical mark of magnoliaceae 35,400,000 years ago and the only ancestor found until now about the vertical evolution of tea plants, offering vegetative basis for citing the native place of tea trees. The hometown of tea is a natural museum of tea trees where there is whole panoply of tea trees (wild type, transition type, and cultivation type) in the world, unfolding a history of civilization about how humans discovered, domesticated, grew and used tea.

The earliest description about tea cultivation along the Lancang River is in *Annals of Yunnan* by Fan Chuo in the Tang dynasty. It is written that peoples living traditionally in Pu'er, Jingdong, Jinggu and south of those areas had grown tea trees over 1,200 years ago (in the period of Nanzhao Kingdom), and they had a special way to make tea and drink it: they cooked tea with Chinese pepper, ginger and cassia bark. Today in the Ancient Tea Plantations of Jingmai Mountain in Pu'er, Yunnan, the native peoples there have adopted a creative way to grow tea trees, namely "the intergrowth of trees and tea plants", creating the tea cultural landscape that "trees, tea plants and humans are in a symbiotic relationship", which has lasted for almost one thousand years and still flourishes. As a result, the Ancient Tea Plantations of Jingmai Mountain was placed on the UNESCO World Heritage Tentative List in 2012. On September 17th, 2023, it gained World Heritage Site status on the 45th World Heritage Committee, a first "tea" -themed Heritage Site in the world.

Pu'er tea, one of the best Chinese teas, got its name just because the Qing government established Pu'er Prefecture in 1729, governing what is now Pu'er, Xishuangbanna and most parts of Lincang where tea was produced, and opened the "tea office" and "main tea store" in charge of issuing tea licenses, levying tea tax and supervising the imperial tea factories. The process of making Pu'er tea is unique: large-leaf tea from Yunnan is made into maocha by withering, fixation, hand rolling and sun-drying; and maocha is made into raw pu'er tea by heating and pressing, and maocha is made into ripe Pu'er tea by heating and pressing after fermentation.

According to *Annals of Pu'er* (1875-1908), Pu'er tea had been sold in the Western Regions and the western frontier zone as early as the Tang dynasty. Pu'er tea comes in such shapes as cake, bowl, brick, and golden melon. Buttered tea the Tibetan love is usually made from tea bricks and bowl-shaped tea which contain tea polyphenols, caffeine, amino acids, vitamins, etc. and not only quench their thirsty and help to digest greasy food but supply the vitamins they lack for their monotonous diet. During the summer investigation in 2022, the proprietor of a Tibetan food restaurant in Benzilan told us, the buttered tea they drink is salty, but the buttered tea in Tibet is sweet with sugar which can relieve altitude sickness.

The Qing government officially put Pu'er tea into file under imperial tea in 1659, and had it carried by horseback to Beijing but it was no longer carried to Beijing from 1839 due to a succession of muggings. In 2005, for the campaign of Pu'er tea culture journey to Beijing — "the Tribute Tea Carried along the Ancient Tea-Horse Road to Beijing by the Caravan", 43 horse drivers from 11 ethnic groups in Yunnan left Ning'er with mobilized 120 pack horses and mules on May 1st, going through Yunnan, Sichuan, Shaanxi, Shanxi, Hebei and Beijing, covering over 4,000 kilometers, arriving in Beijing with over 5 tons of tea in mid-October, and recreating what happened 300 years ago. The Yunnan caravan, travelled gruelingly spreading the caravan culture and donated the money raised where they passed through to build a Hope primary school, and what they have experienced spiritually and achieved physically deserve appreciation and praise.

普洱金瓜茶

Golden Melon-shaped Pu'er Tea

2005 年　云南普洱　直径 33 厘米　高 23 厘米　茶、木质

2005, tea and wood, 33 cm in diameter and 23 cm in height, Pu'er, Yunnan

金瓜茶也称团茶、人头茶，是普洱茶独有的一种特殊紧压茶形式。因其形似南瓜，茶芽长年陈放后色泽金黄，得名金瓜。早年的金瓜茶是专为进贡朝廷而制，故名“金瓜贡茶”。该茶生产始于清代，至今已有 200 多年的历史。此普洱金瓜茶系 2005 年“马帮茶道·瑞贡京城”活动赠送本馆的珍藏品，下有圆形雕花木茶托。

第二单元　马帮用具
Part II　Caravans' Equipment

马帮用具主要包括马帮牌匾，马帮交通、生活、护身用具和常用乐器等。马帮是按民间约定俗成的方式组织起来的一群赶马人及其骡马队的名称。马帮有群、伙、帮之说，一般以九匹马为一群，以三群为一伙，全部骡马放在一起就称之为帮。近代云南大马帮有凤仪帮、蒙化帮、丽江帮等20多支，中小马帮更是数以百计。中央民族大学民族博物馆收藏40余套马鞍、马架、驮具、马铃、马笼头、马尾珠和马尾套等马帮行具，颇具规模，琳琅满目。

Caravans' equipment includes plaques, vehicles and devices, necessities, self-protection tools and musical instruments. The caravan refers to a group of horse drivers and a train of pack animals organized in an unofficially prescriptive way. Generally speaking, a group of 9 horses was called "qun", a group of 3 "qun" called "huo", and a caravan had more than 1 "huo". The big modern Yunnan caravans include over 20 like Fengyi, Menghua, and Lijiang, with hundreds of medium and small-sized caravans. The Museum of Ethnic Cultures, Minzu University of China has a sizably dazzling collection of 40 sets of saddlery like saddles, horseback stands, tools for carrying goods, horse bells, bridles, horsetail beads and horsetail loops.

俗话说，“世上什么苦，赶马做豆腐”。茶马古道滇藏线要穿越复杂的横断山区，为了在艰险的路途上同舟共济，马帮形成了一定的组织形式和许多约定俗成的行为规范。如马帮里有头领马锅头、管事、伙头、马脚子（赶马人）等，越大的马帮组织越严密，拥有上百匹马的马帮，每两匹马配备一名赶马人，配有武装保卫队，马帮要经过少数民族聚居区，还会配备翻译人员。马帮有一定的规矩，包括分配制度、纪律、违反帮规者的惩处办法等。此外，马帮还有行话，是马帮独有的一种语言表达方式，如马帮人称“碗”为“莲花”，因为“碗”和“晚”“完”谐音，不吉利；称“筷子”为“帮手”，因为“筷”和“快”谐音，马帮走太快容易出事故；“闯帮”指两支马帮在狭路上相遇；“开烧”指烧火做饭；“大水”指大量的财物；“开亮”指露宿等。

As the saying goes, “the toiling in the world is driving horses and making tofu.” Yunnan-Tibet route of the Ancient Tea-Horse Road crosses the Hengduan Mountains with complex terrain. Therefore, to pull together in times of trouble, the caravan was organized in a certain way and had a lot of unwritten norms. For example, the caravan had a head called Maguotou, an overseer, cooks, and horse drivers. The bigger caravan, the more highly organized, say, a caravan with over 100 horses would arrange for one horse driver to look after two horses, equipped with armed guards, and translators to facilitate the communication with various peoples. They had rules about income distribution, disciplines, and ways to punish those who broke the rules. Also, they had unique jargon, say, they called “wan” (bowls) “lianhua” (lotus), for “wan”, “wan” (late) and “wan” (screwed) are homophonic, hence inauspicious. “kuaizi” (chopsticks) were called “bangshou” (helper), for “kuai” and “kuai” (fast) are homophonic, and going too fast might cause accidents. “Chuangbang” refers to two caravans encounter on a narrow path; “kaishao” means making a fire to cook; “dashui” means a large amount of property; “kailiang” means camping out, and so on.

一、马帮牌匾 Caravans' Plaques

蒙化马帮牌匾
"Menghua Caravan" Plaque

1937 年　云南　长 156 厘米　宽 42 厘米　厚 4.8 厘米　木质
1937, wood, 156 cm × 42 cm × 4.8 cm, Yunnan

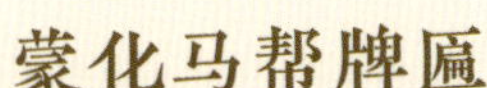

长方形木板，表面以黑漆为底，雕刻出字，再用红漆描字。匾文："蒙化马帮"；落款："哥老会敬送"；年代："民国二十六年"（1937 年）。蒙化为旧县名，今云南大理白族自治州巍山彝族回族自治县、南涧彝族自治县全境。蒙化曾为茶马古道中心以及骡马产地和集中地，因此马帮众多。蒙化马帮是云南 20 多支大马帮中的一支，哥老会是人人皆知的民间帮会组织。蒙化马帮有了哥老会送的牌匾，当地的盗匪便不敢觊觎。抗战时期的蒙化马帮帮助运输抗战物资，为抗战胜利作出了贡献。

二、马帮交通用具 Caravans' Vehicles and Devices

滇马体质结实，短小精悍，善登山越岭，以驮载能力持久见称，故在滇藏茶马古道上组成马帮驮运的多是这种马。除滇马外，实际驮运的则多为骡子，骡子负重和长途跋涉的耐力都优于马。据赶马人说，因为骡子的母体是马，一群骡子里混有几匹马会使它们更听人使唤。马帮交通用具中除了骡马，就是赶马人在驾驭马的时候，为了更方便地控制和保护马匹以及让马看起来健壮而漂亮，所使用的一些辅助器物和装饰品，驮载货物所需要的驮具、储物工具等，主要包括马鞍、马架、驮架和驮包、马垫、马笼头、马嘴套、马镫、马鞭、马尾珠和马尾扣、马衔、铁马掌、马铃、牛铃和各种材质的驮包、筐、箱子、袋子等。

现今巍山大仓镇上饲养的滇马

The Yunnan pony is robust, small but effective, and used to paths in the mountains, with durable load-carrying capability, so it was mostly used as a pack horse on the Yunnan-Tibet route. Besides the pony, the mule was actually preferred, for it is a better stayer than the horse in carrying heavy loads and traveling far. According to the horse driver, it's born by a female horse and a group of mules could be docile with a few horses among them. Besides the pack animals, the horse driver used some accessories to better control, protect and make them look more robust and smarter, and devices for carrying goods and storing things, including saddles, horseback stands, pack racks and pack bags, horse pads, bridles, horse mouth nets, stirrups, whips, horsetail beads and horsetail loops, bits, iron horseshoes, horse bells, ox bells, and panniers, baskets, boxes and sacks.

1. 马鞍　Saddles

马帮使用的马鞍一般都是木胚包牛皮的马鞍。这种普通的马鞍造型单一、工艺简单，在茶马古道上最为常见。这种马鞍的木胚大多为原木色或简单漆成红色。一般来说，彝族、白族的马帮多使用漆饰的马鞍。马鞍上面有大小不一的孔或焊有铁环，便于穿绳固定。其内部为圆弧形，驮在马背不会使马感到难受，外部两头高、中间低的造型，人坐在鞍上也舒适。精致一些的马鞍则是镶银边的。这样的马鞍显示出马锅头的身份、地位和财力。

The caravan's saddles were usually made of wood wrapped in cowhide. These ordinary saddles were simple in form and craft, and very common on the Ancient Tea-Horse Road. The wooden body of this saddle was not painted or just painted red. Generally speaking, the Yi and Bai caravans preferred to use saddles with lacquer finish. A saddle has holes of various size or welded iron rings to thread a rope through for fastening. Its inner is arc-shaped and rests comfortably on the horseback; its outer is shaped like a concave so that one can sit on comfortably. More exquisite saddles go with silver edges, showing the status and wealth of Maguotou.

木马鞍
Wooden Saddle

20 世纪　云南　长 48 厘米　宽 34 厘米　高 26 厘米　木、皮、铁质
The 1900s, wood, leather and iron, 48 cm × 34 cm × 26 cm, Yunnan

马鞍中间有一方孔，侧面有小孔和小铁环，便于系绳固定，正前方内部的边缘部分漆有红漆作为装饰，边缘部分有磨损和裂纹。

红色木马鞍
Red Wooden Saddle

20 世纪　云南　长 50 厘米　宽 26.5 厘米　高 24.5 厘米　木、铁质
The 1900s, wood and iron, 50 cm × 26.5 cm × 24.5 cm, Yunnan

漆成鲜艳的红色，侧面底部有小铁环，便于系绳固定，表面和边缘部分漆脱落和磨损严重。

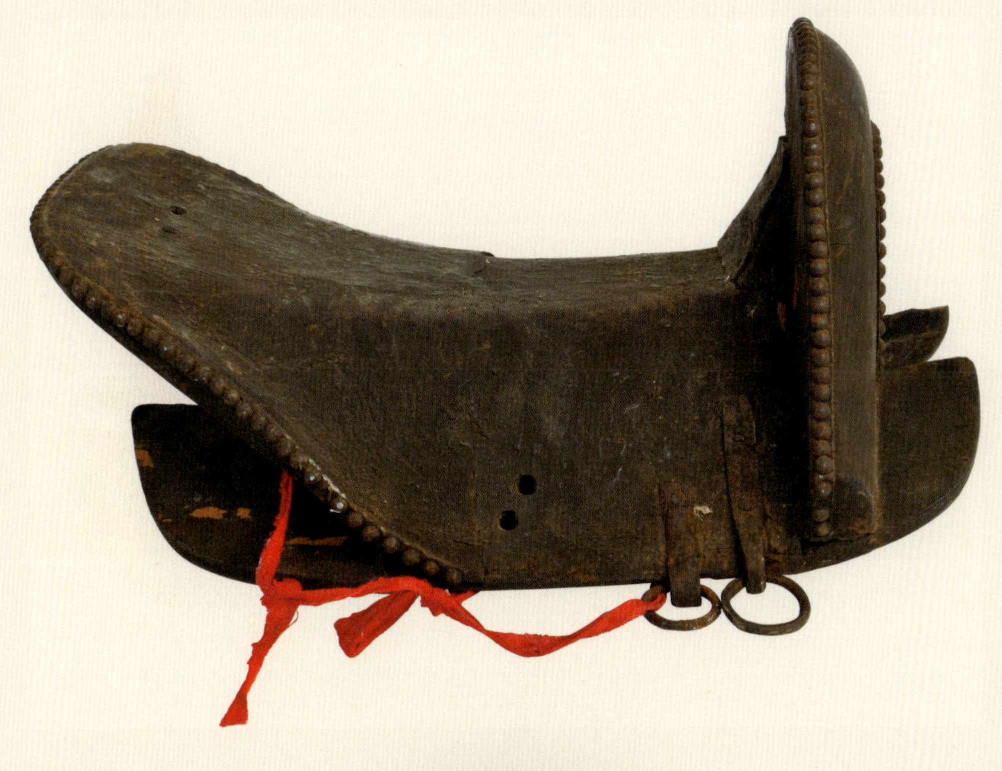

铁珠木马鞍

Saddle Edged with Beads-like Iron Bar

20 世纪　云南　长 48 厘米　宽 32 厘米　高 25.5 厘米　木、铁质

The 1900s, wood and iron, 48 cm × 32 cm × 25.5 cm, Yunnan

前后及内部边缘处用表面呈小珠状的铁条焊接装饰，侧面有小孔和铁环接红绳用于固定，中间已出现裂纹。

镶银木马鞍

Silver-edged Wooden Saddle

20 世纪　云南　长 52.5 厘米　宽 34.3 厘米　高 28 厘米　木、银、铁质

The 1900s, wood, silver and iron, 52.5 cm × 34.3 cm × 28 cm, Yunnan

内部呈弧形，底部有缺损，两侧表面有小铁环，便于系绳固定。前后和内部边缘接口处镶银条装饰，彰显着主人的财富和地位。

2. 马架　Horseback Stands

马架是马帮运输必备的工具，是专门固定在马背上搭载驮架的重要装备，马架上也可以直接捆绑搭载各种货物。马帮在野外宿营时还可将其卸下供马帮人员坐靠休息用。现今巍山永建镇的贺志刚师傅仍在制作马架、驮架等马具，其手艺是他的曾祖父贺应崇传给祖父贺金斗，后又传给他的父亲贺绍彩再传给他的，至今已有四代的传承。

The horseback stand was a must-have device for the caravan to carry goods, placed on the horseback to support a pack rack, or loaded with goods directly. When camping out, the caravan could take it off and put it onto the ground to lean against for a rest. Today, Master He Zhigang in Yongjian Village, Weishan, still makes horseback stands and pack racks, whose craft, starting from his great-great-grandfather, has lasted four generations.

木马架
Wooden Horseback Stand

20 世纪　云南　长 62.5 厘米　宽 34 厘米　高 38.5 厘米　木、铁质
The 1900s, wood and iron, 62.5 cm × 34 cm × 38.5 cm, Yunnan

榫卯结构，为契合马背，内部由木片拼合为弧形，外部两端由木条连接而成，中间小孔处有铁丝，便于固定。

木马架

Wooden Horseback Stand

20 世纪　云南　长 63 厘米　宽 34 厘米　高 39 厘米　木质

The 1900s, wood, 63 cm × 34 cm × 39 cm, Yunnan

中间有小孔便于用绳子固定。为减少摩擦、增加马的舒适度，马架弧形的内部常贴一些如纸壳等柔软的东西。

3. 驮架和驮包　Pack Racks and Pack Bags

驮架是马帮驮运重要的装备，使用时安放在马架上。驮架可以单独使用，也可以和驮包一起使用。驮架还有一种用途，当马帮在外宿营时，可将驮架排列开来，上覆油毡、帆布，人钻入其间便可入睡，既挡风遮雨，又防野兽、蚊虫。

The pack rack was an important device for the caravan to carry goods, placed on the horseback stand when in use. It could be used either alone or together with the pack bags. It also had another use: when the caravan camped out, they could arrange them in a row, cover them with linoleum and canvas, get in and sleep, which was a shelter from the wind and rain as well as from wild beasts and mosquitoes.

木驮架
Wooden Pack Rack

20 世纪　云南　长 77.5 厘米　宽 23.5 厘米　高 46 厘米　木、皮质
The 1900s, wood and leather, 77.5 cm × 23.5 cm × 46 cm, Yunnan

榫卯结构，由木条连接而成，造型呈桥状，简单易制作。驮架上面结实的牦牛皮条用于捆绑物品，下面悬挂的三角形木质锁扣用于扣紧物品。

木驮架

Wooden Pack Rack

20 世纪　云南　长 91 厘米　宽 25 厘米　高 62 厘米　木、皮质

The 1900s, wood and leather, 91 cm × 25 cm × 62 cm, Yunnan

木驮架和皮驮包
Wooden Pack Rack and Leather Pack Bags

20 世纪　云南　长 87 厘米　宽 24 厘米　高 60 厘米　木、皮质
The 1900s, wood and leather, 87 cm × 24 cm × 60 cm, Yunnan

驮架和皮驮包一起使用最为方便。两旁是软皮制成的口袋，驮架上的皮绳用于将装好物品的口袋捆绑系牢在驮架上。

木驮架和铁锅

Wooden Pack Rack and Iron Cooking Pot

20 世纪　云南　长 91.5 厘米　宽 34 厘米　高 68 厘米　木、铁、皮质

The 1900s, wood, iron and leather, 91.5 cm × 34 cm × 68 cm, Yunnan

用皮绳将其捆绑系牢，驮架也可驮运铁锅之类较重的东西。

4. 马垫　Horse Pads

马垫一般有三层：第一层主要是保护马背不被马鞍磨损，选择耐磨的皮子，长宽要与马鞍匹配；第二层要长且宽，几乎要盖住整个马背，能将鞍紧扣其上，起到固定鞍子和保暖、防潮的作用；第三层盖在鞍上，用绳子固定，是骑手的垫子。

The horse pad usually has three layers: the first layer is made of wear-resistant leather matching the size of the saddle so as to protect the horseback from abrasion; the second layer is long and wide, almost covering the whole horseback so that the saddle fits snugly to secure the saddle, keep warm and be moisture-proof; the third layer covers the saddle fixed with a string as the rider's cushion.

獐毛马垫
Roe Deer Furred Horse Pad

20 世纪　云南　长 98 厘米　宽 47 厘米　厚 2 厘米　棉、毛质

The 1900s, cotton and roe deer fur, 98 cm × 47 cm × 2 cm, Yunnan

獐毛马垫为第二层垫子，长度和马身等长，起固定鞍子和保暖、防潮的作用，表面为耐磨柔软的蓝色棉布，呈块状，内装獐子毛。

5. 马笼头 Bridles

马笼头，马帮称辔头，是驾驭和约束马匹必不可少的用具，材质有皮、布、毛线等。其中皮质马笼头耐用结实，最为常用。花笼头色彩艳丽，装饰醒目，是给马帮的头骡和二骡佩戴的。马帮把领头的骡马装扮得漂亮、威风、神气，以提升马帮整体的精气神。

Bridles are indispensable tools for controlling and directing horses, which are made of leather, fabric or wool. But the leather bridle was common for its durability. Bridles with decoration look colorful and eye-catching, only for the leading mule and the second leading mule. The caravan dressed them up so that they looked smart, impressive and vigorous, and further boosting morale among the caravan.

皮马笼头
Leather Bridle

20 世纪　云南　长 45 厘米　宽 18 厘米　高 13 厘米　皮质
The 1900s, leather, 45 cm × 18 cm × 13 cm, Yunnan

将细皮条精细地编成扁平的三股绳，再相互连接成笼头，既结实又贴合马身，方便控制马的行动。

花马笼头
Bridle with Decoration

20 世纪　云南　长 22 厘米　宽 11 厘米　高 62 厘米　皮、棉布、砗磲质

The 1900s, leather, cotton fabric and giant clam, 22 cm × 11 cm × 62 cm, Yunnan

头骡佩戴用，意为骏马开道，妖魔现形，鬼魅快逃。红布上悬挂白色圆形砗磲片，外包彩色毛线边，皮绳上有红色的毛线缨须，用弹簧连接的彩色毛线球，下面连接着棕绳制成的马嘴套。

花马笼头

Bridle with Decoration

20 世纪　云南　长 18 厘米　宽 7 厘米　高 67 厘米　皮、棉布、砗磲质

The 1900s, leather, cotton fabric and giant clam, 18 cm × 7 cm × 67 cm, Yunnan

头骡佩戴用。红布上有三个外包彩色毛线边的白色圆形砗磲片，用弹簧连接的彩色毛线球，下缀红色毛线缨须和棕绳制成的马嘴套。

6. 马嘴套　Horse Mouth Nets

马嘴套具有牵引和控制马匹行动的作用。马是草食动物，茶马古道上两侧青草幽幽，若驮马一边走一边啃食青草，一路慢行必定会误了行程，因此给马套上马嘴套防止它吃草就是必不可少的。马嘴套一般使用耐磨的皮绳和棕绳编织而成。

Horse mouth nets were used to pull and control horses. Horses are herbivorous and there are lush grasses on either side of the path. If pack horses grazed as they went, they would delay the journey. So it was necessary to cover their mouths with the nets, which are made of durable leather or palm fiber strings.

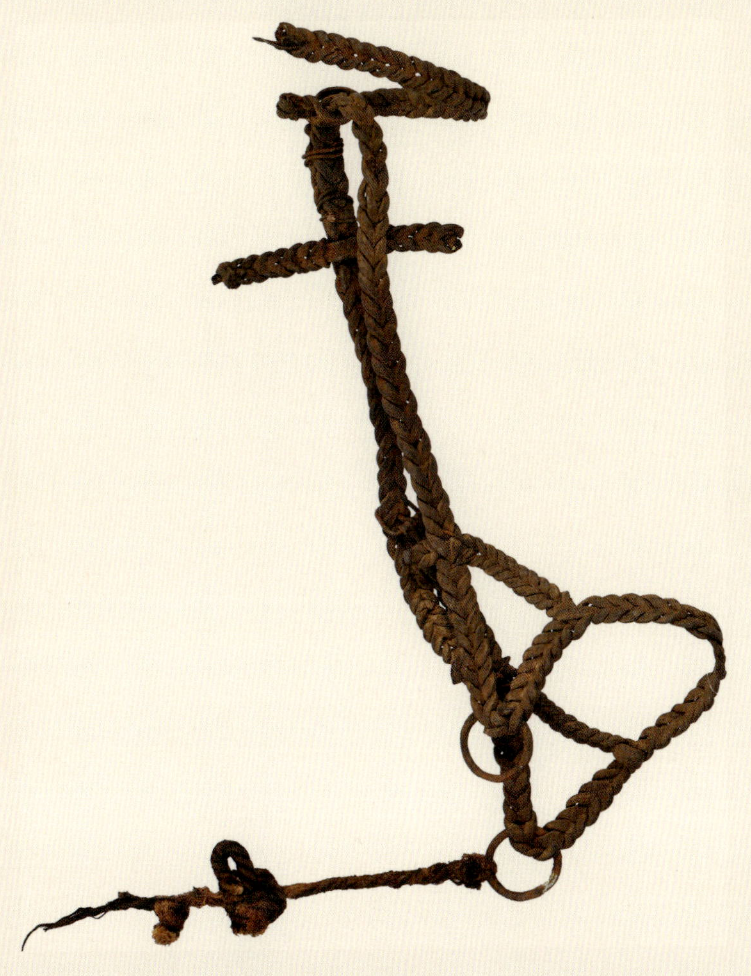

皮马嘴套

Leather Horse Mouth Net

20世纪　云南　长22厘米　宽19厘米　高52厘米　皮质

The 1900s, leather, 22 cm × 19 cm × 52 cm, Yunnan

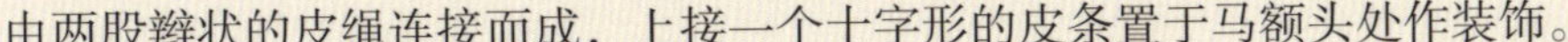

由两股辫状的皮绳连接而成，上接一个十字形的皮条置于马额头处作装饰。

棕马嘴套
Palm Fibered Horse Mouth Net

20 世纪　云南　长 20 厘米　宽 18 厘米　高 19 厘米　绳长 47 厘米　棕纤维质
The 1900s, palm fiber, 20 cm × 18 cm × 19 cm, and 47 cm in string length, Yunnan

由细棕绳编织而成，结实耐用。

7. 马镫　Stirrups

马镫是挂在马鞍两边的脚踏，供赶马人在上下马和骑乘时踏脚，起支撑保护身体的作用。马镫材质可分为铁、铜、藤、皮等。马镫一般是成套出现，金属制成的马镫上都装饰有蝙蝠、祥云、如意结等吉祥图案。茶马古道途经的许多地方都有制作马镫的店铺，为南来北往的马帮提供便利服务。

Stirrups are a pair of pedals that hang down on both sides of a horse's saddle, used to support the horse driver's feet. They are made of iron, copper, rattan or leather. Stirrups appear as one set, Metal stirrups are usually decorated with such patterns as bats, cloud and Ruyi knots. There were many stirrup workshops along the Ancient Tea-Horse Road, facilitating the caravans.

五福捧寿纹铜马镫

Copper Stirrup with Five Bats around the Longevity Symbol

20 世纪　云南　长 14 厘米　宽 7.5 厘米　高 18 厘米　铜、皮质

The 1900s, copper and leather, 14 cm × 7.5 cm × 18 cm, Yunnan

顶端有环形纽用于系绳固定，其下有一只蝙蝠，两翅的末梢凸起，穿孔托住两侧。半圆状的两侧环里各有一只蝙蝠。底部长方形脚踏上两只蝙蝠双翅捧抱一个镂空的“寿”字符，组成了中原文化中广泛流传的“五福捧寿”传统吉祥图案。“蝠”与“福”谐音，五福分指长寿延年、荣华富贵、康乐安宁、行善积德及老年善终，寿则为五福之首。馆藏的这对五福捧寿纹铜马镫实为茶马古道马镫中的精品，体现着中原文化对马帮文化的深刻影响，为民族交往、交流、交融的物证之一。

铁马镫

Iron Stirrup

20 世纪　云南　长 15 厘米　宽 7 厘米　高 19 厘米　铁质

The 1900s, iron, 15 cm × 7 cm × 19 cm, Yunnan

脚踏呈长方形，两侧焊有倒“U”形铁条，顶部有孔，便于穿绳固定。铁马镫是茶马古道上最为常见的马镫。除了长方形脚踏的铁马镫，也有圆形脚踏的铁马镫。

双龙首纹铜马镫

Copper Stirrup with Double Dragon Heads

20 世纪　云南　底径 12 厘米　高 16 厘米　铜质

The 1900s, copper, 12 cm in bottom diameter and 16 cm in height, Yunnan

圆形脚踏，底部中间有五孔，两侧焊有一个倒“U”形的铜环和脚踏相接，铜环顶端有穿孔，便于固定，穿孔上有两个凸起，顶端两侧的一面雕刻双龙首纹饰。

藤马镫
Rattan Stirrup

20 世纪　云南　长 28 厘米　宽 9 厘米　高 22 厘米　藤质
The 1900s, rattan, 28 cm × 9 cm × 22 cm, Yunnan

脚踏处用藤交叉编织而成，两侧用藤编织成半圆形的两个藤环，至后半部中间部分合成一个藤环。藤的表面刷有一层黑漆保护，有的地方已脱落。藤马镫便于携带，非常适合马帮出行。

藤马镫

Rattan Stirrup

20 世纪　云南　长 19 厘米　宽 10 厘米　高 20 厘米　藤质

The 1900s, rattan, 19 cm × 10 cm × 20 cm, Yunnan

8. 马鞭　Horse wipes

马鞭作为传递主人指令的工具，在赶马过程中必不可少，是马具的组成部分。开始，马鞭只是随手拾来的树枝或竹条，后来人们用竹、木或骨等材质制成鞭柄，用皮条或毛线编织成鞭绳。骨质的鞭柄多用牛骨，经过打磨、掏孔、雕刻等工艺制成；木质的鞭柄多为普通木材，也有用红木、紫檀、白根檀等名贵木材制成的。鞭绳一般是由生硬的牛皮芯和狗皮条制成。狗皮编织物松紧适度，富有弹性，是驱赶马的最佳工具。同时马鞭也可作为防身之物。

As a tool to give an order, the horse driver can't go without a horse whip. At first, it was just a picked-up twig or a bamboo rod, and later people used bamboo, wood or bone as a stick, and weaved thongs or wool into strings to make a whip. The common ox bone stick takes the process of polishing, boring and carving; and very few wood sticks are made of precious wood like mahogany, red sandalwood, white rooted sandalwood. The whip string is usually made of hard ox or dog thongs. But the dog-thong-weaved string is preferred for its moderate tightness and good elasticity. In addition, the whip can be used for self-protection.

马鞭

Horse wipe

20 世纪　云南　杆长 39 厘米　鞭长 67 厘米　皮、竹质

The 1900s, leather and bamboo, 39 cm in stick length and 67 cm in string length, Yunnan

由鞭柄和鞭绳两部分组成，竹竿为鞭柄，鞭绳由两条生硬的牛皮芯制成，鞭柄连接处的鞭绳打了几个结，用起来更称手。

9. 马尾珠和马尾扣 Horsetail Beads and Horsetail Loops

马尾珠也称马鞧（音秋），挂在马尾上，一般有骨质、木质和牛角几种，它不仅是漂亮的装饰物，还有实用的功能。当马下坡时，马尾珠可以有效地防止驮架向前滑动和倾斜，起到牵引和固定的作用。磨光且连接成串的大小珠子在上下、左右滚动中还可防止磨伤马的皮毛。马尾扣一般为木质，通常和马尾珠相连，是固定在马尾根部、防止马鞍向前移动的配套工具。

Hung from the horsetail, the beads made of bone, wood or ox horn are not only decorative but practical. When the horse goes downhill, they can prevent the pack rack from slipping forward or tilting. The stringed, polished beads can move up and down and turn right and left so that the skin will not be damaged because of rubbing. The horsetail loop made of wood is linked with the horsetail beads and attached to the top end of the horsetail to stop a saddle from moving forward.

马尾珠和马尾扣
Horsetail Beads and Horsetail Loop

20 世纪　云南　长 17 厘米　宽 3 厘米　高 70 厘米　木、皮质
The 1900s, wood and leather, 17 cm × 3 cm × 70 cm, Yunnan

49 颗木珠下接木质“U”形的马尾扣，用皮绳穿成。有的木珠表面有凹凸的圆圈纹。木珠刷有黑漆保护层，有的已脱落。

马尾珠和马尾扣

Horsetail Beads and Horsetail Loop

20 世纪　云南　长 20 厘米　宽 4 厘米　高 72 厘米　木、皮质

The 1900s, wood and leather, 20 cm × 4 cm × 72 cm, Yunnan

左右各 12 颗木珠，下接木质的“U”形马尾扣，用皮绳穿成。木珠大小基本一样，有的珠子两个连在一起，有的珠子表面有凹凸的圆圈纹。

马尾珠和马尾扣

Horsetail Beads and Horsetail Loop

20 世纪　云南　长 59 厘米　宽 19 厘米　高 3.5 厘米　骨、木、皮质

The 1900s, bone, wood and leather, 59 cm × 19 cm × 3.5 cm, Yunnan

左右各 18 颗骨珠，各自上接一个短骨管，下接木质的“U”形马尾扣，用皮绳穿成。骨珠表面多有凹凸的圆圈纹。

马尾珠和马尾扣

Horsetail Beads and Horsetail Loop

20 世纪　云南　长 64 厘米　宽 18 厘米　高 3 厘米　骨、木、皮质

The 1900s, bone, wood and leather, 64 cm × 18 cm × 3 cm, Yunnan

左右各 18 颗骨珠，各自上接一个短骨管，下接木质的“V”形马尾扣，用皮绳穿成。骨珠表面多有凹凸的圆圈纹。

10. 马衔　Horse Bits

马衔是赶马人和马之间重要的交流媒介，它被放置在马的前切齿之后和后磨齿之前的空当之中，是连接马鼻梁上的铁链、马嚼子和马缰的结合部分。赶马人通过特定的动作使骡马感到舒适是沟通的关键。铜、铁制成的马衔较为常见，除此之外，还有角质和木质的马衔。

It is an important medium of interaction between a horse driver and a horse, which is kept in the gap between the incisors and molars of the horse and a connecting piece of the iron chain on the bridge and the rein. The horse driver controls and directs the horse through given comfortable actions. Though copper and iron bits are common, there are bits made of horn and wood.

马衔
Horse Bit

藏族　20 世纪　云南　长 67 厘米　宽 18 厘米　高 7 厘米　骨、铁、皮质
The 1900s, bone, iron and leather, 67 cm × 18 cm × 7 cm, Tibetan, Yunnan

两羚羊角两端有穿孔，中间有绳相连，连接套马鼻梁上的链子。链子用皮条和小铁环串联而成。

11. 铁马掌　Iron Horseshoes

茶马古道的地形复杂，道路崎岖，骡马负重前行，四蹄易受磨损，必须要给马钉金属的铁马掌。钉马掌是个技术活，需要各种各样的专用工具，如铁掌、铁钉、割削马蹄的铲、钉钉子的榔头、拔马钉的钳子等。行走茶马古道的马帮都会随身携带装有马掌用具的皮囊。滇藏茶马古道重镇巍山至今仍有制作马掌的匠人。

With complex terrain and rugged paths, going heavy-loaded, pack animals' hooves were liable to abrasion. As a result, it was necessary to shoe a horse. Farriery needs skill, and various special tools like iron shoes, iron nails, cutters for cutting a horse's hoof, hammer, and pincers for pulling out a horseshoe nail. The caravan on the Ancient Tea-Horse Road was equipped with leather bags containing the tools for fitting horseshoes. Even today there are farriers in Weishan—a hub on the Yunnan-Tibet route of the Road.

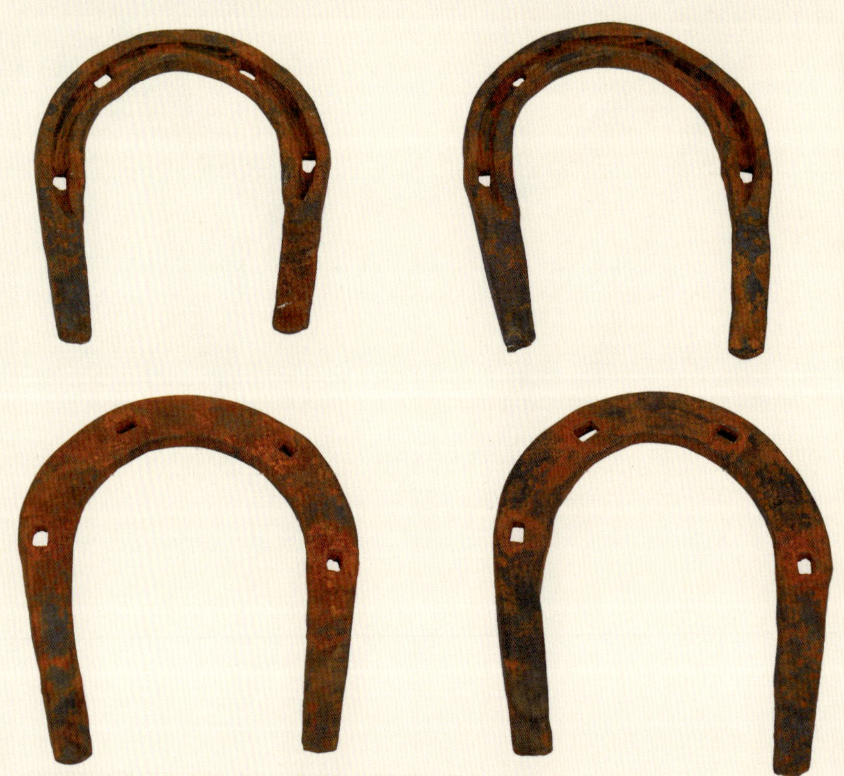

铁马掌
Iron Horseshoes

20 世纪　云南　最长 6 厘米　宽 0.3 厘米　高 8 厘米　铁质
The 1900s, iron, 6 cm in the longest length, 0.3 cm in width and 8 cm in height, Yunnan

铁马掌一般是厚度为 3~4 毫米的生铁，上面有 4~6 个钉眼。“U”形的铁马掌不仅可以起到保护马蹄的作用，还能使马蹄更坚实地抓牢地面，不易打滑。

直角铁铲

Rectangular Iron Cutter

藏族 20世纪 云南 长41厘米 宽18厘米 高0.5厘米 铁质

The 1900s, iron, 41 cm × 18 cm × 0.5 cm, Tibetan, Yunnan

割削马掌的用具。由直的刀柄和直角折成的刀身组成，刀身呈不规则形状，无纹饰，已有锈迹。

12. 马铃　Horse Bells

马帮使用的铃大小不一，形状多样，通常有大铃和小铃之分，有单个的，也有成串的，形状有圆的、方的、筒形的。马铃有以下几种作用：一是赶马人可根据马铃的声响和节奏来检查判断出现问题马匹的位置，从而及时处理。二是马帮在行走途中，头骡戴着一对大铃走在最前面，二骡挂数个小铃紧跟着，形成信号，在狭窄、陡坡的路段，告知对面过来的马帮，注意骡马相互避让，确保双方人马货物的安全。三是在深夜熟睡时，如果马铃声突然乱响，就说明有异常情况发生。此外，马帮还把铃声当作漫长旅途中的一种精神寄托和慰藉。有人给茶马古道清脆、悦耳的马铃声起了个雅号——报君知。马铃声也是爱情的信号，许多凄美动人的马帮爱情故事，就在这“叮当、叮当、叮当”回音悠长的马铃声中传颂回荡着。

Horse bells vary in size and shape (round, square, and cylindrical), some of which are single and some are stringed. They had the following uses: A. the horse driver knew from the ring and rhythm of the bell where the troubled horse was and dealt with it at once; B. when travelling, the leading mule with a pair of big bells walked in front, closely followed by the second leading mule with several strings of small bells, and their bells worked together to signal when they were at narrow or steep parts of the path, informing the approaching caravan should yield for the sake of safety; C. if the bell ran noisily at night, it indicated that something usual happened. Moreover, the caravan took the ring as a spiritual impetus and solace during the long journey and one of them gave the jingle bells an elegant nickname—Baojunzhi. The jingle bell was also a signal of love and a number of moving love stories unfolded with the bells jingling among the mountains.

马帮大铃
Big Bells

20 世纪　云南　长 54 厘米　宽 51 厘米　高 10 厘米　铜、木、棉布质
The 1900s, brass, wood and cotton fabric, 54 cm × 51 cm × 10 cm, Yunnan

为头骡用铃。上为一个圆弧状木片，两头翘起；下部为红布包裹的皮绳，下缀两个大铜铃，铃下有一条窄缝，内有小铁珠，碰之发声，响声粗犷浑厚。

马帮大铃
Big Bells

20 世纪　云南　长 56 厘米　宽 43 厘米　高 9 厘米　铜、木、棉布质
The 1900s, brass, wood and cotton fabric, 56 cm × 43 cm × 9 cm, Yunnan

为头骡用铃。上面圆弧状木片和下面皮绳均用红布包裹，只露出 2 个大铜铃。铜铃除了有裂缝外，还有 4 个小孔，声音洪亮。

马帮大铃
Big Bells

20 世纪　云南　长 60 厘米　宽 50 厘米　高 10 厘米　铜、木、棉布质
The 1900s, brass, wood and cotton fabric, 60 cm × 50 cm × 10 cm, Yunnan

为头骡用铃。上为三角形扁平木片，两头翘起且边缘有沿，可防止下面的铁环脱落。两头边缘处用长皮绳相接，上下用环形铁丝相连，下面皮绳用红布包裹。

马帮大铃

Big Bells

20 世纪　云南　长 63 厘米　宽 47 厘米　高 12 厘米　铜、木、棉布质

The 1900s, brass, wood and cotton fabric, 63 cm × 47 cm × 12 cm, Yunnan

为头骡用铃。上为三角形扁平木片，两头翘起且边缘有沿，可防止下面的皮绳脱落。下面皮绳用红布包裹，铜铃除了有裂缝外，还有小孔。

象纹马帮大铃
Big Bell with Elephant Pattern

20 世纪　云南　直径 12 厘米　高 15 厘米　铜质
The 1900s, brass, 12 cm in diameter and 15 cm in height, Yunnan

为头骡装饰及示警用铃。顶端有环形穿孔，便于穿绳系在骡马颈部，下面圆壳有狭长的裂口，内置一铁丸，一碰发声，声音清亮。底端表面有大象纹饰，与马纹马帮大铃为一对。

马纹马帮大铃
Big Bell with Horse Pattern

20 世纪　云南　直径 12 厘米　高 15 厘米　铜质
The 1900s, brass, 12 cm in diameter and 15 cm in height, Yunnan

为头骡装饰及示警用铃。顶端有环形穿孔，便于穿绳系在骡马颈部，下面圆壳有狭长的裂口，内置一铁丸，一动发声，声音浑厚，底端表面有马纹，与象纹马帮大铃为一对。

马帮小铃
Small Bells

20 世纪　云南　长 52 厘米　宽 46 厘米　高 5 厘米　铜、木、棉布质
The 1900s, brass, wood and cotton fabric, 52 cm × 46 cm × 5 cm, Yunnan

为二骡用铃。上为一个圆弧状木片，两头翘起，中有小孔，用铁条穿过小孔，像扣皮带一样卡住。下面皮绳一个外露，其余的由红布包裹，下缀 5 个小铃。铃下有窄缝，内有小珠，一动即出声，发出的铃声细密清脆。

马帮小铃
Small Bells

20 世纪　云南　长 52 厘米　宽 48 厘米　高 4 厘米　铜、木、棉布质
The 1900s, brass, wood and cotton fabric, 52 cm × 48 cm × 4 cm, Yunnan

为二骡用铃。上为一个圆弧状木片，两端有小孔，用铁条穿过小孔卡住固定。下面皮绳用红布包裹，下缀 5 个小铃。铃下有窄缝，内有小珠，一动即出声。

马帮小铃
Small Bells

20 世纪　云南　长 49 厘米　宽 39 厘米　高 5 厘米　铜、木、棉布质
The 1900s, brass, wood and cotton fabric, 49 cm × 39 cm × 5 cm, Yunnan

为二骡用铃。上为三角形的木条，下面皮绳用红布和麻绳等包裹缠绕，底端缀 8 个兽面纹小铃。

铁马铃

Iron Horse Bell

20 世纪　云南　长 12 厘米　宽 8 厘米　高 25 厘米　铁、木质
The 1900s, iron and wood, 12 cm × 8 cm × 25 cm, Yunnan

为头骡、二骡之外的骡马用铃。筒状，顶端有环状的穿孔，便于系绳固定，内有较为粗大的柱状木槌在铁筒内碰撞，声音浑厚。

铁马铃

Iron Horse Bells

云南 ① 长 9 厘米 宽 6 厘米 高 19 厘米；② 长 8 厘米 宽 5 厘米 高 19 厘米 铁、木质

Iron and wood, ① 9 cm × 6 cm × 19 cm; ② 8 cm × 5 cm × 19 cm, Yunnan

为头骡、二骡之外的骡马用铃。2 个马铃为筒状，大小基本一样，2 个串在一起使用。顶端有环形孔，便于系绳固定，一个内有柱状的木槌，另一个内有钉子状的铁条，碰撞即出声。

13. 牛铃 Ox Bells

茶马古道上并非清一色的骡马队，还有牛帮的存在。一般驮牛 11 头为 1“把”，1 人赶牛；5“把”为小帮（55 头）；牛多至 200~300 头为大帮。每帮有一头身强体壮的头牛，牛头上戴着红绸和镜子，脖子上挂着牛铃。用牛运输的优势在于牛的力气大，许多重物用牛运输要优于骡马。茶马古道的马道多以石头铺垫，牛道则多为土路。牛铃材质多为金属、木质或竹质，簧舌通常为木质或竹质的。给牛佩戴牛铃，一是让主人通过铃声来确定牛走的方位，二是有节奏的铃声停止或无序时，主人就会马上发现问题并能及时处理。至今云南许多地方仍给牛佩戴牛铃，方便主人寻找。

Besides the caravan with horses and mules, caravans with oxen traveled along the Ancient Tea-Horse Road. Generally, a group of 11 pack oxen was called a “ba”, taken care of by one driver; five “ba” formed a small caravan (with 55 oxen); as many as 200-300 oxen formed a big caravan. Each caravan had a robust leading ox, its head wearing a ribbon of red silk and a mirror, and with a bell hung from its neck. The ox could do better job in terms of heavy loads because of its greater strength. The bridle paths of the Ancient Tea-Horse Road were stone-paved, but the ox paths were not surfaced. The ox bell was made of metal, wood or bamboo, and its clapper was made of wood or bamboo. With the ox bell, the owner could know where the oxen were, and would react immediately when the bell stopped sounding or sounded arrhythmic. Even today, the ox bells are used in many parts of Yunnan, so that the oxen will be easily located.

木牛铃
Wooden Ox Bell

20 世纪　云南　长 27 厘米　宽 8 厘米　高 12 厘米　木、铁、布质
The 1900s, wood, iron and fabric, 27 cm × 8 cm × 12 cm, Yunnan

长方形，两端有柱状凸起，便于系绳悬挂于牛脖颈处。内有两个柱状的木质簧舌，上有铁丝帮助固定，碰撞出声，声音浑厚。

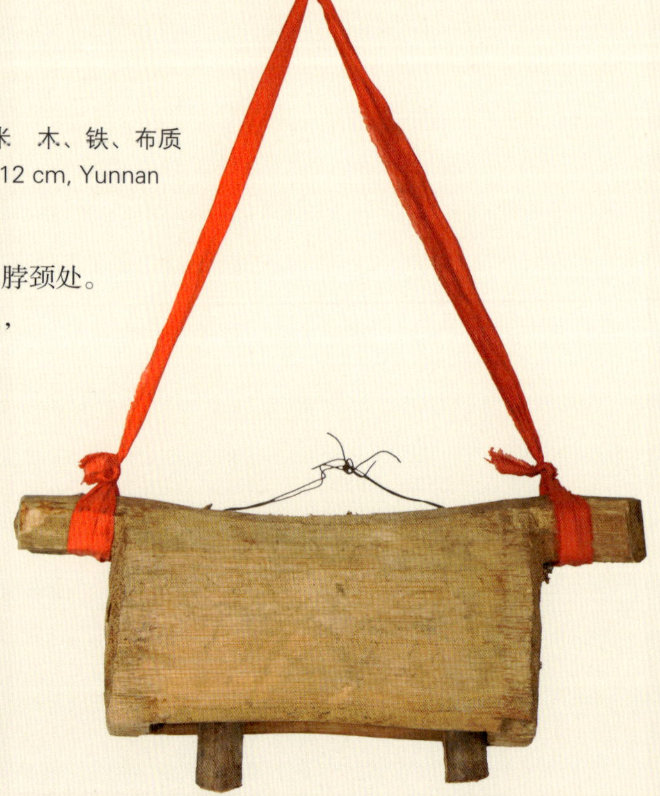

木牛铃

Wooden Ox Bell

20 世纪　云南　长 25 厘米　宽 7.5 厘米　高 12 厘米　木、皮质

The 1900s, wood and leather, 25 cm × 7.5 cm × 12 cm, Yunnan

长方形，两端有柱状凸起，上系皮绳，可套于牛脖颈处。内有两个柱状的木质簧舌，碰撞出声。

带木架铜牛铃

Brass Ox Bell with Wooden Frame

20 世纪　云南　长 31 厘米　宽 16 厘米　高 31 厘米　铜、木质

The 1900s, brass and wood, 31 cm × 16 cm × 31 cm, Yunnan

两边为倒“U”形木架，木架由铁丝固定，结实牢固，其中有一个小圆锥形木质锁扣。居中有扁钟，内带木槌，撞击时声音浑厚悦耳，韵味十足。

带木架铜牛铃

Brass Ox Bell with Wooden Frame

20 世纪　云南　长 34 厘米　宽 15 厘米　高 30 厘米　铜、木质

The 1900s, brass and wood, 34 cm × 15 cm × 30 cm, Yunnan

14. 储物工具　Storage Tools

茶马古道上，用于装货物的储物工具形制多样，有竹、藤、皮、铁、木、麻等材质做成的袋子、包、筐、篓、柜、箱和桶等。其中大大小小的皮包，尤其是皮褡裢，因耐磨、结实且防潮，既可以装日用品，也可以装食物和货物，很受青睐。褡裢过去通常是指我国民间长期使用的一种长方形、中间开口的口袋，里面放东西，出门时可将它搭在肩上，空出两手方便行动。马帮的皮褡裢一般放在驮架上使用。

驮架上的皮褡裢和竹筐里的树舌灵芝

On the Ancient Tea-Horse Road, the storage tools for carrying goods come in a wide variety of kinds such as sacks, bags, baskets, boxes, cases, and buckets, made of bamboo, rattan, leather, iron, wood or hemp. Of all the bags, panniers were the most popular, because they were durable, damp-proof, and could be used for carrying not only daily necessities but food and goods. The pannier had meant a long, rectangular bag sewn up at both ends with an opening in the middle, usually worn across the shoulder to facilitate the user's action with his or her hands taking nothing. Yet the pannier of the caravan mostly sat on the load rack.

翻盖皮褡裢

Clamshell Leather Pannier

20 世纪　云南　长 62 厘米　宽 35 厘米　高 30 厘米　皮质

The 1900s, leather, 62 cm × 35 cm × 30 cm, Yunnan

由皮拼接而成，两边开口，翻盖分两层，内层有搭扣，中间有一个连接，夹层有木板用作造型，两侧有圆形的扣襻。

翻盖皮褡裢

Clamshell Leather Pannier

20 世纪　云南　长 73 厘米　宽 40 厘米　高 34 厘米　皮质

The 1900s, leather, 73 cm × 40 cm × 34 cm, Yunnan

翻盖皮褡裢

Clamshell Leather Pannier

20 世纪　云南　长 56 厘米　宽 37 厘米　高 37.5 厘米　皮质

The 1900s, leather, 56 cm × 37 cm × 37.5 cm, Yunnan

双层翻盖，锁边，两侧各有两个圆皮圈，下压缀皮条，皮条可伸入下面的金属锁扣中扣住，避免包内物品漏出。

牦牛皮包
Yak Hide Bag

20 世纪　云南　长 46 厘米　宽 22 厘米　高 69 厘米　皮质
The 1900s, leather, 46 cm × 22 cm × 69 cm, Yunnan

筒状，口端处穿有细皮条，用于收紧袋口，防止东西漏出。底部再垫一皮条防止磨损漏底。

牦牛皮包

Yak Hide Bag

20 世纪　云南　长 42 厘米　宽 21 厘米　高 78 厘米　皮质

The 1900s, leather, 42 cm × 21 cm × 78 cm, Yunnan

筒状，口端处穿有细皮条，用于收紧袋口，防止东西漏出。中间两侧还有皮条帮助固定。

牦牛皮包
Yak Hide Bag

20 世纪　云南　长 48 厘米　宽 16 厘米　高 57 厘米　带长 98 厘米　穗长 50 厘米　皮质
The 1900s, leather, 48 cm × 16 cm × 57 cm, 98 cm in strap length and 50 cm in fringe length, Yunnan

皮包口端有孔可穿绳束紧，边缘留有许多流苏状细皮条作为装饰，中间有一条长皮带用于背挎或系驮架上。

竹篾筐

Bamboo Strip Basket

20 世纪　云南　长 58 厘米　宽 42 厘米　高 39 厘米　竹质

The 1900s, bamboo, 58 cm × 42 cm × 39 cm, Yunnan

椭圆形口，由几种粗细不同的竹篾编织而成，中间部分为双层，内层细密，外层疏朗，交叉编织出不同的图案。

圆竹筐

Round Bamboo Basket

20 世纪　云南　长 29 厘米　宽 20 厘米　高 33.5 厘米　竹质

The 1900s, bamboo, 29 cm × 20 cm × 33.5 cm, Yunnan

由细竹条编织而成，上部有一圈凸出来的浅沿，应该有盖，已遗失。

带盖圆竹筐

Round Bamboo Basket with Cover

20 世纪　云南　直径 48 厘米　高 31.5 厘米　竹质

The 1900s, bamboo, 48 cm in diameter and 31.5 cm in height, Yunnan

盖和筐体由粗细不同的两种竹条编织而成，筐中间和底部都留有许多空隙，便于空气的流通，可用来装运活禽等。

方形竹油笼

Square Bamboo Oil Container

20 世纪　云南　长 51.5 厘米　宽 29.5 厘米　高 49 厘米　竹质

The 1900s, bamboo, 51.5 cm × 29.5 cm × 49 cm, Yunnan

圆口平底。先用细竹条编织成形后，用矿石做干燥剂。把猪血、石灰、香油按一定的比例，温度保持在 90℃左右熬成浓缩的油料。熬上一两天后，用手工棉纸分两层涂裱，再刷上苋油后晾干，一只油笼就做成了。做好后，它既可以装油，也可以装水，马帮就经常使用它来驮水、装油。

圆形竹油笼

Round Bamboo Oil Container

20 世纪　云南　口径 15 厘米　底径 24 厘米　高 40 厘米　竹质

The 1900s, bamboo, 15 cm in opening diameter, 24 cm in bottom diameter and 40 cm in height, Yunnan

圆直口，圆腹平底，用细竹条编织而成。油笼既可以用来装油，也可以装水。

翻盖竹筐

Clamshell Bamboo Basket

20 世纪　云南　长 42 厘米　宽 27 厘米　高 43 厘米　竹质
The 1900s, bamboo, 42 cm × 27 cm × 43 cm, Yunnan

由粗细两种竹条交替编织成双层竹筐，前面焊有铁质“8”字形扣条和环形扣襻，背面有铁环和环形扣襻连接，一角处有竹节制成的足，用于支撑和固定。

翻盖竹筐

Clamshell Bamboo Basket

20 世纪　云南　长 44 厘米　宽 27 厘米　高 39 厘米　竹质

The 1900s, bamboo, 44 cm × 27 cm × 39 cm, Yunnan

上半部分由粗细竹条编织而成，细竹条在里，粗竹条在外起保护作用；下半部分由细竹条编织而成，粗竹条垫底，使之耐磨结实。前面有铁质扁圆形扣条和环形扣襻，两旁有两个小铁环便于固定。竹节做的足已有缺失。

翻盖竹筐
Clamshell Bamboo Basket

20 世纪　云南　长 44 厘米　宽 26 厘米　高 38 厘米　竹质
The 1900s, bamboo, 44 cm × 26 cm × 38 cm, Yunnan

由粗细不同的几种竹条编织成两层的筐，内层细密，外层有的细密，有的稀疏，编织出图案和花纹。翻盖接口处由粗竹条箍紧，前面有铁质长方形扣条和环形扣襻。

翻盖竹篾筐

Clamshell Bamboo Strip Basket

20 世纪　云南　长 50 厘米　宽 34 厘米　高 38 厘米　竹质
The 1900s, bamboo, 50 cm × 34 cm × 38 cm, Yunnan

由细竹篾条编织而成，边缘处用厚竹片包裹。前面有铁质“8”字形扣条和环形扣襻，背面有大小铁环组成的扣襻，底部有竹节制成的四足。

翻盖竹编提篮

Clamshell Bamboo Basket with Strap

20 世纪　云南　长 37 厘米　宽 18 厘米　高 23 厘米　绳长 51 厘米　竹质

The 1900s, bamboo, 37 cm × 18 cm × 23 cm and 51 cm in strap length, Yunnan

由细竹丝编织成双层，内层细密，外层疏朗，用不同的编织方法，编织出镂空的图案和花纹。边缘、中间和底部用厚竹片包裹保护，两侧有竹编的穿孔，上系布带方便手提和背挎。

翻盖竹编提篮
Clamshell Bamboo Basket with Strap

20 世纪　云南　长 36 厘米　宽 19 厘米　高 25 厘米　绳长 50 厘米　竹质

The 1900s, bamboo, 36 cm × 19 cm × 25 cm and 50 cm in strap length, Yunnan

竹篾箱

Bamboo Strip Box

20 世纪　云南　长 61 厘米　宽 40 厘米　高 42.5 厘米　竹质
The 1900s, bamboo, 61 cm × 40 cm × 42.5 cm, Yunnan

内由细篾条平行细密编织而成，外用粗厚的竹片编织成正方形框架来加固保护，正面有金属的锁扣和小挂锁，足为竹节制成，已有缺损。

带盖竹篾箱

Bamboo Strip Box with Cover

20 世纪　云南　长 43.5 厘米　宽 29.5 厘米　高 50 厘米　竹、木质

The 1900s, bamboo and wood, 43.5 cm × 29.5 cm × 50 cm, Yunnan

由粗细不同的篾条用多种手法编织而成。竹篾箱的上下两端都绑有木条，在搬运和运输的过程中能对箱子起到很好的保护作用，适宜茶马古道上的长途运输。

竹篾箱

Bamboo Strip Box

20 世纪　云南　长 48 厘米　宽 34.3 厘米　高 45 厘米　竹质

The 1900s, bamboo, 48 cm × 34.3 cm × 45 cm, Yunnan

由粗细不同的篾条用不同的手法编织而成。竹篾箱前面有铁质的扣和扣襻，顶端有两条宽竹片便于手提，边缘处用粗厚的竹片包裹保护。四足由竹节制成。

红漆木箱

Red Lacquer Wooden Box

20 世纪　云南　长 73 厘米　宽 42 厘米　高 30 厘米　木、铁质

The 1900s, wood and iron, 73 cm × 42 cm × 30 cm, Yunnan

前面有铁质的扣和扣襻，一侧有半圆形铁质耳，另一侧铁质耳已缺失，表面边缘和局部红漆已脱落。

双耳包皮木箱

Double-handled Leather-wrapped Box

20 世纪　云南　长 66 厘米　宽 41.6 厘米　高 27.2 厘米　木、铁、皮质
The 1900s, wood, iron and leather, 66 cm × 41.6 cm × 27.2 cm, Yunnan

前面有铁质的扣和扣襟，两侧有铁质耳，整个木箱用黄色皮子包裹后再用黑色的铁皮包裹四角，避免磕碰。表面有磨损和破损。

双耳包皮木箱

Double-handled Leather-wrapped Box

20 世纪　云南　长 65.5 厘米　宽 41.6 厘米　高 27.2 厘米　木、铁、皮质

The 1900s, wood, iron and leather, 65.5 cm × 41.6 cm × 27.2 cm, Yunnan

前面有铁质的扣和扣襻，两侧有铁质耳，整个木箱用红色皮子包裹后再用黑色铁皮和铆钉包裹四角，避免磕碰。

双耳铁皮箱

Double-handled Iron Box

20 世纪　云南　长 70 厘米　宽 40 厘米　高 26 厘米　铁质

The 1900s, iron, 70 cm × 40 cm × 26 cm, Yunnan

前面有 3 个卡口，扣好后非常严实，两侧有耳，表面有 3 条凸起的脊，结实耐磨。

锥形木片拼大桶

Conical Bucket

20 世纪　云南　长 43.5 厘米　宽 30.5 厘米　高 71 厘米　木、竹质

The 1900s, wood and bamboo, 43.5 cm × 30.5 cm × 71 cm, Yunnan

由下窄上宽的木片拼接成锥形，外面用数圈竹条箍紧。

双柄木片拼大桶

Double-handled Bucket

20 世纪　云南　长 53 厘米　宽 36.5 厘米　高 60 厘米　木、竹、铁质

The 1900s, wood, bamboo and iron, 53 cm × 36.5 cm × 60 cm, Yunnan

桶身由木片拼接而成，中间用竹条，底部用细铁丝箍紧，两侧有方形带孔的柄，方便手拿和固定。

麻袋
Sack

20世纪　云南　长106厘米　宽73厘米　麻质
The 1900s, hemp, 106 cm × 73 cm, Yunnan

麻织的袋子。因为轻便且容量大，是茶马古道上最实用、最常见的储物工具。

三、马帮生活 The Life of Caravans

(一) 衣 Costumes

1. 披毡 Felt Capes

茶马古道滇藏线冬长夏短，在赶马路途中，服装的防寒保暖对身体是非常重要的。羊毛擀制的披毡、毡片，外形古朴，既可以随身携带抵挡风寒，还能晚上当被盖取暖。披毡最早源于古代的羌人，郭义恭《广志》上记载羌人"女披大华毡以为盛饰"，从中可知当时羌女子以披有大而华丽的披毡为盛装。披毡后来在我国彝族、藏族中较为常见。

With short summer and long winter on the Yunnan-Tibet route of the Tea-Horse Road, it was very important for the members of the caravan to be dressed in warm clothes while traveling. Felt capes and sheets of primitive simplicity, made from a mass of wool by rolling and pressing, could be used as quilts at night as well as warm clothes. The cape originated from the ancient Qiang people, and *the Record of Produce* by Guo Yigong reads, "A woman wearing a big felt cape is thought to dress up." So the Qiang women took the felt capes as their Sunday best. Later, the felt capes were common among the Yi and Tibetan peoples.

黑披毡
Black Felt Cape

藏族　20 世纪　云南　长 170 厘米　宽 117 厘米
毛毡质

The 1900s, felt, 170 cm × 117 cm, Tibetan, Yunnan

黑色羊毛擀制而成，圆形下摆，领口处用绳系紧，有两处破损。

黑披毡

Black Felt Cape

藏族 20 世纪 云南 长 156 厘米 宽 82 厘米 毛毡质

The 1900s, felt, 156 cm × 82 cm, Tibetan, Yunnan

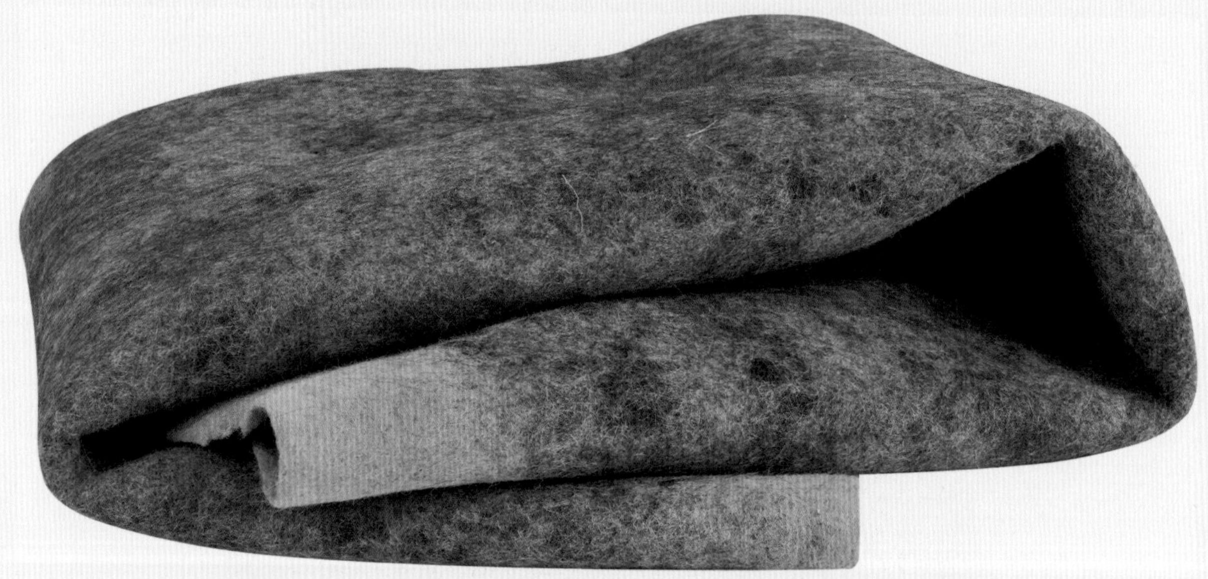

白毡垫
White Felt Mat

藏族　20 世纪　云南　长 170 厘米　宽 108 厘米　毛毡质
The 1900s, felt, 170 cm × 108 cm, Tibetan, Yunnan

片状，由白色羊毛擀制而成。藏族马帮野外露营时垫坐，睡觉时当毯。

黑毡垫
Black Felt Mat

藏族　20 世纪　云南　长 230 厘米　宽 136 厘米　毛毡、毛发质
The 1900s, felt and hair, 230 cm × 136 cm, Tibetan, Yunnan

由黑色羊毛和少部分毛发混合擀制而成。

2. 皮坎肩　Leather Sleeveless Jackets

皮坎肩穿脱方便，材质耐磨结实，挡风舒适。皮坎肩正面下方有口袋，背面的下摆处有长条的储物空间，非常实用方便。麂皮坎肩制作精细，是马帮服饰中的精品。

Made of durable leather, the sleeveless jackets were easy to put on or take off and comfortably sheltered from the wind. With a pocket at either low side of the front and a long storage space at its back hem, the jacket was quite practical. Exquisitely made of muntjac deer leather, the sleeveless jackets were the best of the caravan's clothes.

棕色皮坎肩
Brown Leather Sleeveless Jacket

20 世纪　云南　身长 58 厘米　肩宽 34 厘米　下摆 61 厘米　皮质
The 1900s, leather, 58 cm in length, 34 cm in shoulder width and 61 cm in hem length, Yunnan

领口、前襟、下摆、口袋上方和肩袖连接处皮条包边，前襟两组盘扣。背面下摆处有长条的储物袋，方便储物。

白色麂皮坎肩

White Muntjac Deer Leather Sleeveless Jacket

20 世纪　云南　身长 62 厘米　肩宽 36 厘米　下摆 50 厘米　麂皮质

The 1900s, muntjac deer leather, 62 cm in length, 36 cm in shoulder width and 50 cm in hem length, Yunnan

前襟有七排盘扣，口袋上方有倒葫芦状的翻盖及扣襻，均由手工缝制，背面下摆处有长条的储物袋，保暖性、安全性和装饰性俱佳。

白色麂皮坎肩
White Muntjac Deer Leather Sleeveless Jacket

20 世纪　云南　身长 62 厘米　肩宽 36 厘米　下摆 50 厘米　麂皮质
The 1900s, muntjac deer leather, 62 cm in length, 36 cm in shoulder width and 50 cm in hem length, Yunnan

前襟有 5 排盘扣，2 个口袋上方有 4 个倒葫芦状的小翻盖设计，上下有扣襻，突出了装饰和安全性，背面下摆处有长条的储物袋。

白色麂皮坎肩

White Muntjac Deer Leather Sleeveless Jacket

20 世纪　云南　身长 62 厘米　肩宽 36 厘米　下摆 50 厘米　麂皮质

The 1900s, muntjac deer leather, 62 cm in length, 36 cm in shoulder width and 50 cm in hem length, Yunnan

前襟有手工缝制的十排细密盘扣，2 个口袋上方有 4 个倒葫芦状的小翻盖设计，让这件麂皮坎肩的保暖性、安全性和装饰性都趋于完美，只是一肩部已有破损，另一肩打有补丁。

3. 蓑衣和斗笠 Straw Rain Capes and Bamboo Hats

蓑衣和斗笠是较为常见的马帮避雨工具。长年行走在茶马古道上的马帮人把蓑衣和斗笠随时备于身边，用它们为人马遮挡烈日和风雨，蓑衣还可作为夜里防潮的睡垫。

The straw rain capes and bamboo hats were common tools for the caravan to shelter from the rain. Travelling along the Ancient Tea-Horse Road all the year round, members of the caravan kept them close, using them against the burning sun, the wind and rain, and the cape was also used as a damp-proof sleeping pad at night.

草蓑衣
Straw Rain Cape

20 世纪　云南　长 87 厘米　高 111 厘米　草质
The 1900s, straw, 87 cm × 111 cm, Yunnan

里面织成网状，穿上扁平舒适，外面的草保持原始状态，修剪成形，接触雨水后会顺势而下，不会渗进去打湿衣服。

竹斗笠

Bamboo Hat

20 世纪　云南　直径 48 厘米　高 12 厘米　竹质

The 1900s, bamboo, 48 cm in diameter and 12 cm in height, Yunnan

顶端用线缝制一个五角星形状的装饰物，既好看，又可防止顶端漏雨。斗笠又称“笠帽”，呈圆锥形，多为竹质，竹斗笠上刷上一层油可防雨。

竹斗笠

Bamboo Hat

20 世纪　云南　直径 45.2 厘米　高 13 厘米　竹质
The 1900s, bamboo, 45.2 cm in diameter and 13 cm in height, Yunnan

4. 皮挎包　Leather Shoulder Bags

皮革缝制的赶马人的随身挎包，是用来装钱币、针线和一些重要物件的小包，经久耐用，是当年行走在茶马古道的马帮人必备的行头。

Sewn of durable leather, the small shoulder bag was used to carry money, sewing kit, and something important, which was a must-have outfit for the horse driver traveling along the Ancient Tea-Horse Road.

皮挎包
Leather Shoulder Bag

藏族　20 世纪　云南　长 46 厘米　宽 14 厘米　高 50 厘米　皮质
The 1900s, leather, 46 cm × 14 cm × 50 cm, Tibetan, Yunnan

开口处有小孔，穿有皮条，方便束口，中间有一皮条可用来背挎，下面流苏状的皮条用于装饰。

皮挎包
Leather Shoulder Bag

藏族　20 世纪　云南　长 46 厘米　宽 14 厘米　高 50 厘米　皮质
The 1900s, leather, 46 cm × 14 cm × 50 cm, Tibetan, Yunnan

开口处留有穿皮条的孔，皮条已遗失，两边有皮条连接，可以用来背挎。

5. 护身符　Amulets

藏族马帮中的赶马人大多信仰藏传佛教和自然宗教。佛像、佛盒（嘎乌）、猴头骨、真言八卦纹等挂饰，是这些马帮人出门必须携带的护身符。这些护身符的材质有铜、泥、银、皮、木、骨等。佛盒里面一般装有小佛像、经书、从释迦牟尼佛像上换下来的佛衣一角以及活佛的衣角、药物等。藏族民间认为，这些护身符是万能吉祥之物，虔诚佩戴，便可时时得到神佛的护佑。这小小的挂件里寄托了他们的精神追求，承载着他们对平安、财富、吉祥、顺利的期望。

Most of the horse drivers in the Tibetan caravan believed in Tibetan Buddhism and natural religion. Pendants like Buddha figurine, Ga'u box, monkey skull, mantra and the Eight-trigram were amulets. The caravan men must take with them when leaving home. The amulets are made of brass, clay, silver, leather, wood, and bone. Ga'u box contains Buddha figurine, scripture, a bit of the dress taken off from the statue of Sakyamuni and a bit of the living Buddha's dress, and medication. The Tibetan people believed that these amulets were omnipotent and auspicious, and as long as one wore them piously, one would get bless from Buddha. These little pendants symbolize their spiritual quest and embody their desire for peace, wealth, auspiciousness and going smoothly.

带皮套铜佛像护身符
Brass Buddha Amulet with Leather Case

藏族　20 世纪　云南　长 9 厘米　宽 0.3 厘米　高 12 厘米　绳长 25 厘米　皮、铜质
The 1900s, leather and brass, 9 cm × 0.3 cm × 12 cm and 25 cm in string length, Tibetan, Yunnan

带皮套铜佛像护身符
Brass Buddha Amulet with Leather Case

藏族　20 世纪　云南　长 9 厘米　宽 0.5 厘米　高 12 厘米　绳长 25 厘米　皮、铜质

The 1900s, leather and brass, 9 cm × 0.5 cm × 12 cm and 25 cm in string length, Tibetan, Yunnan

彩漆泥塑黄财神护身符

Painted Clay Figurine Amulet of Yellow Jambhala

藏族　20 世纪　云南　长 11 厘米　宽 3 厘米　高 13 厘米　绳长 27 厘米　泥、皮质

The 1900s, clay and leather, 11 cm × 3 cm × 13 cm and 27 cm in string length, Tibetan, Yunnan

彩绘泥塑文殊护身符
Painted Clay Figurine Amulet of Manjusri

藏族　20 世纪　云南　长 10 厘米　宽 2 厘米　高 12 厘米　绳长 25 厘米　泥、皮质
The 1900s, clay and leather, 10 cm × 2 cm × 12 cm and 25 cm in string length, Tibetan, Yunnan

彩绘泥塑长寿佛护身符

Painted Clay Figurine Amulet of Amitayus

藏族　20 世纪　云南　长 10.5 厘米　宽 3 厘米　高 11 厘米　绳长 22 厘米　泥、皮质

The 1900s, clay and leather, 10.5 cm × 3 cm × 11 cm and 22 cm in string length, Tibetan, Yunnan

八宝纹银嘎乌盒

Silver Ga'u Box with Eight Treasure Pattern

藏族　20 世纪　云南　长 8.5 厘米　宽 4 厘米　高 11 厘米　绳长 15 厘米　银、麻质

The 1900s, silver and hemp, 8.5 cm × 4 cm × 11 cm and 15 cm in string length, Tibetan, Yunnan

带布套八宝纹银嘎乌盒

Silver Ga'u Box with Eight Treasure Pattern and Cloth Case

藏族　20 世纪　云南　长 8.5 厘米　宽 4 厘米　高 10 厘米　绳长 53 厘米　银、布质

The 1900s, silver and fabric, 8.5 cm × 4 cm × 10 cm and 53 cm in string length, Tibetan, Yunnan

带布套八宝纹银嘎乌盒

Silver Ga'u Box with Eight Treasure Pattern and Cloth Case

藏族　20 世纪　云南　长 8 厘米　宽 4.5 厘米　高 10 厘米　绳长 48 厘米　银、布质

The 1900s, silver and fabric, 8 cm × 4.5 cm × 10 cm and 48 cm in string length, Tibetan, Yunnan

带布套八宝纹银嘎乌盒
Silver Ga'u Box with Eight Treasure Pattern and Cloth Case

藏族　20世纪　云南　长8厘米　宽4厘米　高8厘米　绳长47厘米　银、布质

The 1900s, silver and fabric, 8 cm × 4 cm × 8 cm and 47 cm in string length, Tibetan, Yunnan

带布套八宝纹银嘎乌盒

Silver Ga'u Box with Eight Treasure Pattern and Cloth Case

藏族　20 世纪　云南　长 9 厘米　宽 4.5 厘米　高 9 厘米　绳长 50 厘米　银、布质

The 1900s, silver and fabric, 9 cm × 4.5 cm × 9 cm and 50 cm in string length, Tibetan, Yunnan

带布套八宝纹银嘎乌盒

Silver Ga'u Box with Eight Treasure Pattern and Cloth Case

藏族　20 世纪　云南　长 8 厘米　宽 4 厘米　高 12 厘米　绳长 48 厘米　银、布质

The 1900s, silver and fabric, 8 cm × 4 cm × 12 cm, and 48 cm in string length, Tibetan, Yunnan

彩绘木雕顶髻佛母像挂饰

Painted Wood Carving Pendant of Ushnishavijaya

藏族　20 世纪　云南　长 15 厘米　宽 2 厘米　高 25 厘米　木质

The 1900s, wood, 15 cm × 2 cm × 25 cm, Tibetan, Yunnan

彩绘木雕佛像挂饰
Painted Wood Carving Pendant of Buddha

藏族 20 世纪 云南 长 15 厘米 宽 2 厘米 高 24 厘米 木质
The 1900s, wood, 15 cm × 2 cm × 24 cm, Tibetan, Yunnan

彩绘木雕佛像挂饰

Painted Wood Carving Pendant of Buddha

藏族　20 世纪　云南　长 15 厘米　宽 2 厘米　高 23 厘米　木质

The 1900s, wood, 15 cm × 2 cm × 13 cm, Tibetan, Yunnan

猴头骨挂饰

Monkey Skull Pendant

藏族　20 世纪　云南　长 15 厘米　宽 2 厘米　高 23 厘米　骨、角、玛瑙质

The 1900s, bone, horns and agate, 15 cm × 2 cm × 23 cm, Tibetan, Yunnan

主要由猴头骨制成，头骨上有骨质的两个尖角，从头骨顶上穿孔，将 12 颗红玛瑙珠子，4 块扁平的、上有圆圈纹的骨片和 6 颗小骨珠穿成挂饰。猴头骨挂饰据说有辟邪的作用，适宜马帮出门携带。

真言八卦纹铜挂饰

Brass Pendant with Mantra and the Eight-trigram

藏族 20 世纪 云南 长 7.3 厘米 宽 1.2 厘米 高 7 厘米 铜质

The 1900s, brass, 7.3 cm × 7 cm × 1.2 cm, Tibetan, Yunnan

挂饰一面中间为藏文六字真言，另一面中间为中原道家的九宫八卦图，可见内地文化对藏族马帮的深刻影响，真言八卦纹挂饰成为反映民族交往、交流、交融的物证之一。

（二）食　Food

1. 炊具　Cooking Utensils

马帮常年在路上，行进中做饭是必不可少的。马帮的炊具材质以铜、铁为主，馆藏有铜锣锅、铁锅、吊锅、蒸桶以及小糕甑子等。铜锣锅与马帮的许多习俗禁忌有关，马帮的领队“马锅头”这一称呼的来历也和锣锅有关。马帮吃饭时，马锅头须坐在饭锣锅的正对面，面对要走的方向，锣锅煮熟的饭，第一口必须由他来盛和吃，所以便有了“马锅头”之称，这是权力，也是责任的象征。还有一些其他的讲究，如打翻盛了米或焖好饭的锣锅，被视为犯大忌；盛饭的时候要用手按住锣锅，不能使其翻转；用勺在锅里盛饭时，不能直接挖成一个洞，要一层一层地舀出来等。茶马古道重镇巍山是中国名小吃之乡，这里还有一个美丽的民间故事。传说巍山古城内有一个马锅头喜好甜食，尤其喜欢吃米糕。心灵手巧的妻子就发明出便于携带、制作方便的蒸小糕用具小糕甑子，让远行的丈夫能在赶马的长途跋涉中，享受到那份带着浓浓思念的甜蜜和慰藉。

Cooking was essential for the caravan on the way all the year round. Their cooking utensils were chiefly made of copper and iron, such as copper pots, iron pots, hanging pots, steaming casks and small rice cake steaming pot in the museum collection. The copper pots are associated with the caravan's customs and taboos, for example, the title “Maguotou”, head of the caravan, came from the pot. When eating, Maguotou must sit right opposite the pot with rice, facing the direction in which they would go. He was always the first person to get the cooked rice from the pot and eat, hence the title, “Maguotou”, a symbol of power and responsibility. There were some taboos, for example, overturning the pot with cooked rice was seen as one of them; when getting rice, one should hold the pot steady so as not to tip it; one could not scoop out a hole in the cooked rice with a ladle but take out layer by layer. Weishan—a hub on the Tea-Horse Road—is well-known for snacks in China, and there goes a beautiful folk tale: a Maguotou in the old town of Weishan loved desserts, especially rice cake. So his ingenious wife invented an easy-to-carry and user-friendly steamer for small rice cake in order to let her husband be able to enjoy the cake full of deep passion and comfort while traveling far.

带盖提梁红铜锣锅

Copper Pot with Lid and Arc Handle

20 世纪　云南　口径 23 厘米　底径 23 厘米　高 17.5 厘米　铜质

The 1900s, copper, 23 cm in opening diameter, 23 cm in bottom diameter, 17.5 cm in height, Yunnan

煮食用具。铜锣锅是茶马古道上最常用的炊具，一般用铜锻造而成，上小下大，上半部分如一个小铜盆倒扣成盖，下半部分向外鼓起呈圆形，有单梁可吊起来当吊锅用，用它煮出来的饭菜香甜可口。

带盖提梁白铜锣锅

Copper Pot with Lid and Arc Handle

20 世纪　云南　口径 20 厘米　底径 20 厘米　高 17.5 厘米　铜质

The 1900s, copper, 20 cm in opening diameter, 20 cm in bottom diameter, 17.5 cm in height, Yunnan

煮食用具。此锣锅双耳延伸至底部，可防止锣锅变形。

双耳铁锅

Iron Pot with Double Rings

20 世纪　云南　口径 37.3 厘米　腹径 39 厘米　高 24 厘米　铁质

The 1900s, iron, 37.3 cm in opening diameter, 39 cm in major diameter, and 24 cm in height, Yunnan

煮食用具。口沿内折后外撇，双耳，鼓腹，便于持拿，也可用绳吊起使用。

双耳铁吊锅

Hanging Iron Pot with Double Rings

20 世纪　云南　口径 22.5 厘米　腹径 24.7 厘米　高 17.6 厘米　铁质

The 1900s, iron, 22.5 cm in opening diameter, 24.7 cm in major diameter, and 17.6 cm in height, Yunnan

煮食用具。带盖，盖顶焊有环状的纽，双耳，鼓腹，有一个铁丝做的提梁，可吊起使用。

四系铁锅

Iron Pot with Four Rings

20 世纪　云南　口径 23 厘米　腹径 24.7 厘米　高 18 厘米　铁质

The 1900s, iron, 23 cm in opening diameter, 24.7 cm in major diameter, and 18 cm in height, Yunnan

煮食用具。带盖，鼓腹，盖顶焊有环状的纽。有 4 个小耳，带孔，方便穿绳作为吊锅使用。

铁锅
Iron Pot

20 世纪　云南　口径 47 厘米　腹径 36 厘米　高 40.5 厘米　铁质
The 1900s, iron, 47 cm in opening diameter, 36 cm in minor diameter, and 40.5 cm in height, Yunnan

煮食用具。敞口、宽沿、深腹，烧水和煮食物时不易溢出。

圆口铜罐

Copper Pot with Round Opening

20 世纪　云南　口径 14 厘米　腹径 22 厘米　底径 20 厘米　高 20 厘米　铜质

The 1900s, copper, 14 cm in opening diameter, 22 cm in major diameter, 20 cm in bottom diameter, and 20 cm in height, Yunnan

煮食用具。圆直口，深腹平底。

陶小糕甑子

Pottery Small Rice Cake Steaming Pot

20 世纪　云南　单口径 7.8 厘米　底径 19.5 厘米　高 17 厘米　陶质

The 1900s, pottery, 7.8 cm in opening diameter (per hole), 19.5 cm in bottom diameter, and 17 cm in height, Yunnan

蒸小糕用具。小糕松软爽口，是巍山的传统小吃。锅盖上有 2~3 个洞眼，备好相应数量的木质小圆甑卡置在锅盖洞眼上。大米经过淘、洗、泡、舂等工序加工成糕面。小圆甑内装入糕面，蒸两三分钟后，在其中一甑糕面上抹上芝麻、红糖，再把另一甑糕翻扣在上面，继续蒸一两分钟后，两块合一的小糕就可以食用了。人们说这是合起来的甜蜜。

五格陶火锅

Pottery Hot Pot with Five Partitions

20 世纪　云南　口径 44.5 厘米　高 17 厘米　陶质

The 1900s, pottery, 44.5 cm in diameter and 17 cm in height, Yunnan

煮食用具。折沿平底，不同的食品分在不同的格子里煮，味道不会混在一起搅乱味觉，而且能够节省烹饪时间，适合马帮出行人多时使用，可满足不同的口味。

双耳木蒸桶

Wooden Steaming Cask with Double Square Handles

20 世纪　云南　单口径 7.8 厘米　底径 19.5 厘米　高 17 厘米　木质

The 1900s, wood, 7.8 cm in opening diameter, 19.5 cm in bottom diameter, and 17 cm in height, Yunnan

蒸食用具。中空，底部有一个十字架形状的木质垫底，上面放蒸格，外表面有用木条和铁钉修补的痕迹，两侧有方形的把手，便于手持。

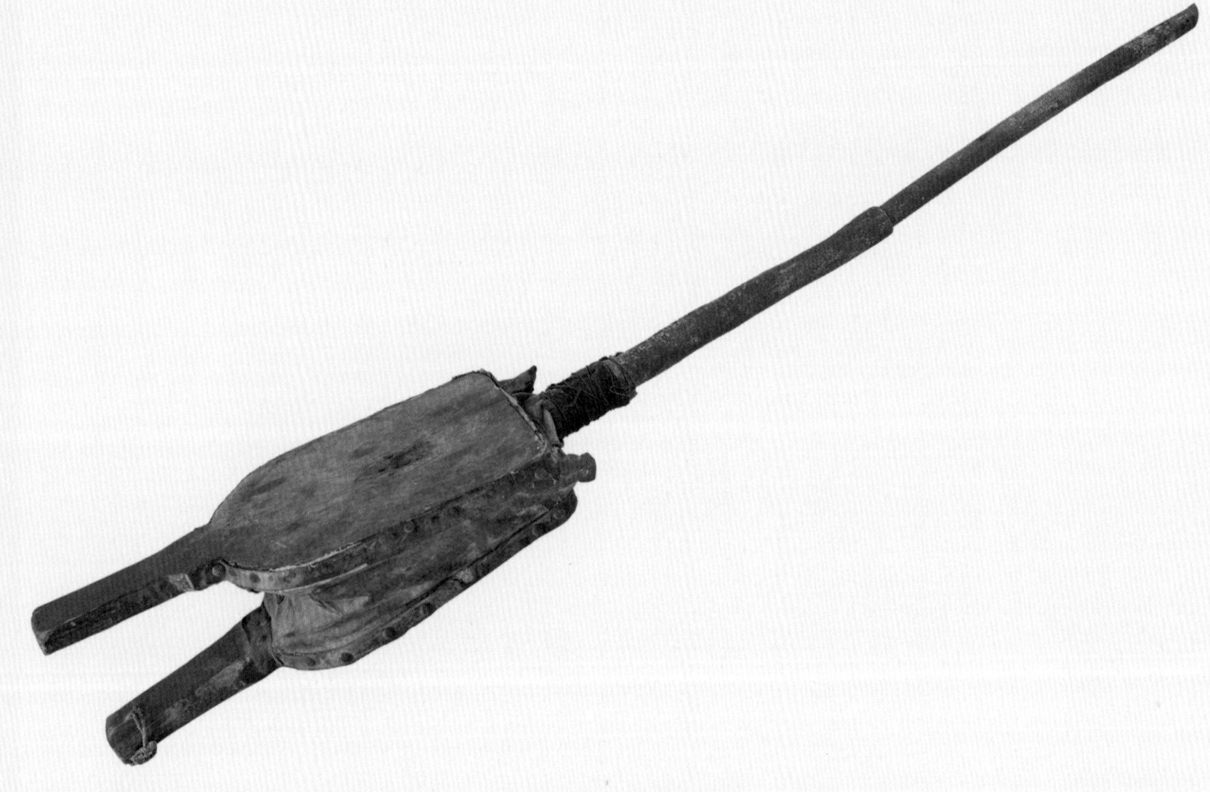

铁管皮囊木鼓风机

Wooden Bellows with Leather Bag and Iron Tube

藏族　20 世纪　云南　长 108 厘米　宽 15 厘米　高 22 厘米　木、铁、皮质
The 1900s, wood, iron and leather, 108 cm × 15 cm × 22 cm, Tibetan, Yunnan

鼓风吹火工具。由鼓风囊和通风管两部分构成，鼓风囊上有两个相对的木质手柄，其中的一面上有一圆口，中间夹一皮囊，通过两手柄不断地开合，将产生的风通过通风管送到助燃点助燃。藏族马帮野外宿营遇到雨雪天气时，就用这种工具来助燃生火。

2. 渔具　Fishing Gear

马帮在行进途中，遇到溪河湖泊等水面，时常会用随身携带的竹编鱼篓来捕鱼捞虾，这不仅可以改善膳食、增加营养，还可以丰富生活、增加情趣。

When caravans came across rivers or lakes where there were fish, they would catch fish and shrimp with bamboo fish traps that they carried along, which not only theat themselves, increase nutrition but also enrich their life, spice things up.

竹编鱼篓
Bamboo Fish Trap

20 世纪　云南　底径 9 厘米　高 24 厘米　竹质
The 1900s, bamboo, 9 cm in bottom diameter and 24 cm in height, Yunnan

用细竹条编织而成。鱼篓设计为双层，内层不到头，底部中空，鱼进入夹层后就不易逃出。两侧有穿孔，便于系绳携带。

竹编鱼篓
Bamboo Fish Trap

20 世纪　云南　底径 8.5 厘米　高 21 厘米　竹质
The 1900s, bamboo, 8.5 cm in bottom diameter and 21 cm in height, Yunnan

3. 餐具　Dishware and Cutlery

行走在路上的马帮经常风餐露宿，在野外使用的餐具要便于携带、易清洗。馆藏马帮餐具有碗套、碗、油瓶、壶、调料罐等，材质有藤、竹、金属、陶瓷等。碗放入一个竹藤编制的碗套里，而餐刀和筷子组合放在一起，这样既可以保护餐具，有保洁作用，携带和使用也非常方便，体现了马帮人的生活智慧。

The travelling caravan often ate and slept in the open and the utensils should be easy to carry and wash. The museum collection includes bowl cases, bowls, oil bottles, pots, seasoning jars, which are made of rattan, bamboo, metal or ceramic materials. Bowls were kept in bamboo or rattan cases and knives and chopsticks together but separately from the bowls, so they were kept undamaged and sanitary, and easy to carry and use, which shows the caravan's life wisdom.

椭圆形竹篾碗套
Bamboo Strip Oval Bowl Case

20 世纪　云南　长 16 厘米　宽 13 厘米　高 7 厘米　竹质
The 1900s, bamboo, 16 cm × 13 cm × 7 cm, Yunnan

装碗用具。用竹中抽出的细篾条编织而成，分上下两层，套在一起使用，容易脱落，用麻绳系牢。外面刷有一层黑漆保护膜。

圆藤碗套
Round Rattan Bowl Case

20 世纪　云南　直径 19 厘米　高 9 厘米　藤质
The 1900s, rattan, 19 cm in diameter and 9 cm in height, Yunnan

装碗用具。用细藤条编织而成。分上下两层，边缘有沿，方便套在一起。其内外都刷有黑漆保护膜，并用麻绳来系牢。

圆藤碗套
Round Rattan Bowl Case

20 世纪　云南　口径 14.5 厘米　底径 6 厘米　高 8 厘米　藤质

The 1900s, rattan, 14.5 cm in opening diameter, 6 cm in bottom diameter, and 8 cm in height, Yunnan

装碗用具。用藤条编织而成。分上下两层，边缘有沿，方便套在一起。顶部有凹陷，中心有一小圆孔，直通到底，一侧有绳状的扣襻，两侧都有细藤条帮助束紧碗套，便于携带。

嵌瓷片藤碗套

Rattan Bowl Case Inlaid with Tile

20 世纪　云南　长 13 厘米　宽 12 厘米　高 7 厘米　藤、瓷质

The 1900s, rattan and porcelain, 13 cm × 12 cm × 7 cm, Yunnan

装碗用具。用细藤条编织而成。六边形，一侧有盘扣，另一侧有十字形的连接。黑漆为底色，在锁扣和棱处刷红漆，颜色对比和谐亮丽，顶端镶嵌有呈八瓣花形的青花瓷片。嵌瓷原为广东潮汕汉族的民间传统装饰工艺，历史可追溯至明代万历年间，迄今已有 400 多年历史。青花瓷片上有缠枝菊花纹饰。菊花在中原文化中被誉为花中四君子之一，它代表的君子文化是中华民族独特的精神标识。菊花凌霜而开，傲岸不屈，象征着中华民族正直不屈的民族精神，同时也象征着吉祥长寿。嵌瓷片藤碗套也是茶马古道上反映民族交往、交流、交融的物证之一。

藤碗套
Rattan Bowl Case

20 世纪　云南　直径 11 厘米　高 12 厘米　藤质
The 1900s, rattan, 11 cm in diameter and 12 cm in height, Yunnan

装碗用具。用细藤条编织而成。圆形，分上下两层，顶端有一个圆形薄凸起，一侧有盘扣，另一侧有连接。内刷黑漆保护，外刷间隔的黑红两色漆，对比分明，别致好看。

青花瓷碗

Blue and White Porcelain Bowl

20 世纪　云南　口径 13.2 厘米　底径 8 厘米　高 4.7 厘米　瓷质

The 1900s, porcelain, 13.2 cm in opening diameter, 8 cm in bottom diameter, and 4.7 cm in height, Yunnan

敞口，弧腹，圈足，内有不规则的几何图案。碗内和碗底一圈无釉是挂釉时摞烧工艺留下来的，它可避免碗与碗之间黏结。摞烧工艺烧造产量高，成本低。

青花瓷碗

Blue and White Porcelain Bowl

20 世纪　云南　口径 13.2 厘米　底径 5.9 厘米　高 5.1 厘米　瓷质

The 1900s, porcelain, 13.2 cm in opening diameter, 5.9 cm in bottom diameter, 5.1 cm in height, Yunnan

敞口，弧腹，圈足，内有青花图案，碗底一圈无釉。因坯没有干就烧制，以至碗有些变形。

白釉瓷碗

White-glazed Porcelain Bowl

20 世纪上半叶　云南　口径 16 厘米　底径 6.3 厘米　高 5.6 厘米　瓷质

The 1st half-1900s, porcelain, 16 cm in opening diameter, 6.3 cm in bottom diameter, and 5.6 cm in height, Yunnan

敞口，弧腹，圈足，施釉不均，多处有瑕疵，边缘部分漏胎。因坯没有干就烧制，边缘部分向内凹陷，碗已经变形。

青花瓷小碟

Blue and White Porcelain Saucer

20 世纪中期　云南　口径 10 厘米　底径 4.6 厘米　高 3.4 厘米　瓷质

The mid-1900s, porcelain, 10 cm in opening diameter, 4.6 cm in bottom diameter, and 3.4 cm in height, Yunnan

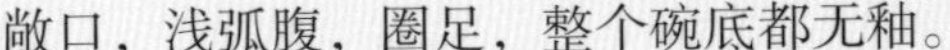

敞口，浅弧腹，圈足，整个碗底都无釉。

蒙古刀鞘筷子

Mongolian Knife with Sheath and Chopsticks

20 世纪　云南　长 35.5 厘米　宽 4 厘米　骨、钢质

The 1900s, bone and steel, 35.5 cm × 4 cm, Yunnan

刀把雕刻云卷纹，刀鞘雕刻婴戏图，套上有醒目的金属箍用于保护和装饰。骨质的刀鞘，可以插小刀和筷子，使用方便。中原文化中的婴戏图寓意多子多福，生活美满。此餐具在内蒙古牧区较为流行，方便放牧和赶马使用，是茶马古道上各民族交往、交流、交融的物证之一。赶马人的刀鞘筷子一般和火镰、鼻烟壶放一起，挂在腰间，是身份的象征。

金粉彩绘木糌粑盒

Gilt Painted Wooden Zanba Box

藏族 20 世纪 云南 口径 4.5 厘米 腹径 15 厘米 底径 9 厘米 高 13 厘米 木质

The 1900s, wood, 4.5 cm in opening diameter, 15 cm in major diameter, 9 cm in bottom diameter, and 13 cm in height, Tibetan, Yunnan

盛糌粑用具。分上下两层，上为塔形盖，绘有龙纹，下为钵形的底，绘有“卍”字吉祥图案。糌粑是用青稞炒制磨成的炒面，与酥油茶、酸奶等捏成团吃，是藏族的主食。糌粑盒藏语称“巴拉”，常见的是红色，有木质、铜质等多种，其中以树根雕刻的糌粑盒为上乘。糌粑放盒里可起到防潮、防虫和保鲜的作用。

带盖木盒

Wooden Box with Cover

藏族　20 世纪　云南　长 20 厘米　宽 10 厘米　高 22 厘米　绳长 28 厘米　木、皮质

The 1900s, wood and leather, 20 cm × 10 cm × 22 cm and 28 cm in strap length, Tibetan, Yunnan

桶形，一侧有木质穿孔，另一侧木质穿孔已破损，改用铁丝穿孔，上系皮绳为梁。带盖木盒实用且轻便，易于携带，被广泛用于茶马古道。

青釉瓷油壶

Blue-glazed Porcelain Oil Pot

20世纪早期　云南　口径6.5厘米　底径10.6厘米　高25厘米　瓷质

The early-1900s, porcelain, 6.5 cm in opening diameter, 10.6 cm in bottom diameter, and 25 cm in height, Yunnan

盘口有流，口沿内折，细颈，平肩，深腹，平底且施釉不均匀。

青釉弦纹瓷油壶
Blue-glazed Porcelain Oil Pot with String Pattern

20 世纪早期　云南　口径 4.3 厘米　底径 10 厘米　高 19 厘米　瓷质

The early-1900s, porcelain, 4.3 cm in opening diameter, 10 cm in bottom diameter, and 19 cm in height, Yunnan

盘口有流，口沿内折，细颈，平肩，深腹，平底，腹部下方有数条弦纹。

褐釉弦纹瓷油瓶

Brown-glazed Porcelain Oil Bottle with String Pattern

20 世纪前期　云南　口径 3.5 厘米　底径 3.8 厘米　高 11 厘米　瓷质

The early-1900s, porcelain, 3.5 cm in opening diameter, 3.8 cm in bottom diameter, and 11 cm in height, Yunnan

盘口有流，唇内折，细颈，平肩，鼓腹，圈足，上有均匀的弦纹。

褐釉陶油瓶
Brown-glazed Pottery Oil Bottle

20 世纪前期　云南　口径 4.1 厘米　底径 4 厘米　高 10.3 厘米　陶质
The early-1900s, pottery, 4.1 cm in opening diameter, 4 cm in bottom diameter, and 10.3 cm in height, Yunnan

侈口，短颈，球形腹，圈足，瓶身残留把的痕迹。

褐釉弦纹陶油瓶

Brown-glazed Pottery Oil Bottle with String Pattern

20 世纪前期　云南　口径 3.6 厘米　底径 4.2 厘米　高 10.3 厘米　陶质

The early-1900s, pottery, 3.6 cm in opening diameter, 4.2 cm in bottom diameter, and 10.3 cm in height, Yunnan

---

唇口，溜肩，细颈，鼓腹，有数条弦纹，平底且施釉不到底。

黄褐釉弦纹陶壶

Yellowish Brown-glazed Pottery Pot with String Pattern

20 世纪前期　云南　口径 8.5 厘米　底径 12 厘米　高 33.5 厘米　陶质

The early-1900s, pottery, 8.5 cm in opening diameter, 12 cm in bottom diameter, and 33.5 cm in height, Yunnan

唇口内折，防止液体外流，平口，细颈，鼓腹，平底，底部有缺损。

黄褐釉弦纹陶壶

Yellowish Brown-glazed Pottery Pot with String Pattern

20 世纪前期　云南　口径 6.5 厘米　底径 11 厘米　高 23 厘米　陶质

The early-1900s, pottery, 6.5 cm in opening diameter, 11 cm in bottom diameter, and 23 cm in height, Yunnan

平口，折沿，细颈，深腹，平底且施釉不到底，上塞玉米芯做的盖。

乳白釉弦纹细颈瓷壶

Narrow-necked Opal-glazed Porcelain Pot with String Pattern

20 世纪前期　云南　口径 6.5 厘米　底径 10 厘米　高 26 厘米　瓷质

The early-1900s, porcelain, 6.5 cm in opening diameter, 10 cm in bottom diameter, and 26 cm in height, Yunnan

盘口，有流，细颈，鼓腹，平底且施釉不到底，颈部下方系绳，便于携带。

绿釉瓷盐罐
Green-glazed Porcelain Salt Jar

20 世纪中期　云南　口径 8 厘米　底径 11 厘米　高 13 厘米　瓷质
The mid-1900s, porcelain, 8 cm in opening diameter, 11 cm in bottom diameter, and 13 cm in height, Yunnan

直口，口沿内折，口沿和底部露胎，球形腹，平底且施釉不到底。盖已遗失。

绿釉三联瓷调料罐
Green-glazed Triple Porcelain Seasoning Jar

20 世纪 50 年代　云南　单口径 7.6 厘米　单底径 3.3 厘米　宽 15.5 厘米　高 5.5 厘米　瓷质

The 1950s, porcelain, 7.6 cm in opening diameter (per jar), 3.3 cm in bottom diameter (per jar), 15.5 cm in width, and 5.5 cm in height, Yunnan

唇口，束颈，鼓腹，平底。内施釉不均，仅口沿处有釉。外施釉不到底，底部露胎。

4. 酒具　Drink Vessels

艰辛劳顿的马帮在山道中急行，酒是赶马人解乏去困的上好饮料。马帮酒具的材质主要为木、竹和陶瓷。其颈部通常细长，在马帮的行进过程中，酒不易溢出。

During a long, arduous journey, Chinese liquor was the best drink to remove fatigue for the horse driver. The caravan's drink vessels are mainly made of wood, bamboo and ceramic materials. They are normally narrow-necked and the liquor does not spill easily on the way.

竹套木瓶
Wooden Bottle with Bamboo Case

20 世纪　云南　口径 6 厘米　底径 13 厘米　高 34 厘米　木、竹质
The 1900s, wood and bamboo, 6 cm in opening diameter, 13 cm in bottom diameter, 34 cm in height, Yunnan

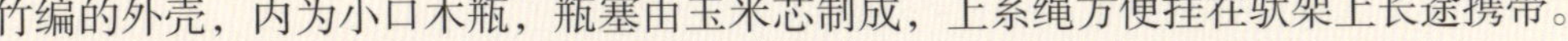

竹编的外壳，内为小口木瓶，瓶塞由玉米芯制成，上系绳方便挂在驮架上长途携带。

提梁竹筒
Bamboo Tube with Arc Handle

20 世纪　云南　口径 14 厘米　底径 12 厘米　高 32 厘米　绳长 15 厘米　竹、皮质

The 1900s, bamboo and leather, 14 cm in opening diameter, 12 cm in bottom diameter, 32 cm in height, and 15 cm in string length, Yunnan

由竹节制成，已有裂纹，上系皮绳为梁，轻便、易于携带，被广泛用于茶马古道。

深褐釉绳纹陶壶
Dark Brown-glazed Pottery Pot with Rope Pattern

20 世纪前期　云南　口径 6.5 厘米　底径 13.5 厘米　高 28 厘米　陶质
The early-1900s, pottery, 6.5 cm in opening diameter, 13.5 cm in bottom diameter, and 28 cm in height, Yunnan

小喇叭口，细长颈，深腹上布满绳纹，平底。

乳白釉绳纹陶壶
Opal-glazed Pottery Pot with Rope Pattern

20 世纪前期　云南　口径 6.5 厘米　底径 11 厘米　高 32.5 厘米　陶质
The early-1900s, pottery, 6.5 cm in opening diameter, 11 cm in bottom diameter, and 32.5 cm in height, Yunnan

盘口，细颈，橄榄形深腹上布满绳纹，平底。

黄褐釉弦纹陶壶

Yellowish Brown-glazed Pottery Pot with String Pattern

藏族　20 世纪前期　云南　口径 9 厘米　底径 13.5 厘米　高 37 厘米　陶质

The early-1900s, pottery, 9 cm in opening diameter, 13.5 cm in bottom diameter, and 37 cm in height, Tibetan, Yunnan

直口，唇口，下垂沿，细颈，溜肩，鼓腹，平底。

绿釉高足陶酒杯
High-foot Green-glazed Pottery Drinking Cup

20 世纪　云南　口径 7 厘米　底径 6 厘米　高 10 厘米　陶质
The 1900s, pottery, 7 cm in opening diameter, 6 cm in bottom diameter, and 10 cm in height, Yunnan

直口，弧腹，高足，平底，高足杯因便于单手把杯，也称把杯。

绿釉高足陶酒杯

High-foot Green-glazed Pottery Drinking Cup

20 世纪　云南　口径 7 厘米　底径 6 厘米　高 10 厘米　陶质

The 1900s, pottery, 7 cm in opening diameter, 6 cm in bottom diameter, and 10 cm in height, Yunnan

5. 茶具 Tea Set

马帮常年行走在崇山峻岭之间，夜间宿营或中途休息时，通常会泡一壶茶慢慢品饮，享受这难得的休闲时光，既可以消除疲劳，又可去火提神。马帮的茶具材质主要为陶瓷和金属，馆藏有装茶叶的陶瓷罐，用来烧水泡茶、盛茶的茶壶等。

The caravan travelled among jagged mountains throughout the year, and when camping at night or stopping over they would make tea to sip, enjoying the valuable leisure time, which could relieve fatigue, remove heatiness and refresh themselves. Their tea set was mainly made of ceramic and metal materials. The collection includes ceramic jars for holding tea, kettles for boiling water, and teapot for making or serving tea.

乳白釉双系瓷罐

Opal-glazed Porcelain Jar with Double Rings

20 世纪前期　云南　口径 9 厘米　底径 8.6 厘米　高 16 厘米　瓷质

The early-1900s, porcelain, 9 cm in opening diameter, 8.6 cm in bottom diameter, and 16 cm in height, Yunnan

装茶叶用具。直口，圆唇，口沿内折，矮颈，鼓腹，平底且施釉不到底。

绿釉双系瓷罐

Green-glazed Porcelain Jar with Double Rings

20 世纪中期　云南　口径 8.6 厘米　底径 8 厘米　高 14.5 厘米　瓷质

The mid-1900s, porcelain, 8.6 cm in opening diameter, 8 cm in bottom diameter, and 14.5 cm in height, Yunnan

装茶叶用具。平口，削肩，深腹，内施白色釉，平底且施釉不到底。

带盖提梁铜壶

Copper Kettle with Lid and Arc Handle

20 世纪　云南　口径 15 厘米　底径 18 厘米　高 20 厘米　铜质

The 1900s, copper, 15 cm in opening diameter, 18 cm in bottom diameter, and 20 cm in height, Yunnan

烧水用具。带环形纽壶盖，敛口，肩鼓，收腹，平底，口沿多处有缺口。壶盖和壶体之间有绳相连，可避免壶盖丢失。有两根粗铁丝做成的提梁，简单实用，为茶马古道上最常见的茶壶。

带盖提梁铜壶
Copper Kettle with Lid and Arc Handle

20 世纪　云南　口径 7.7 厘米　底径 12 厘米　高 11 厘米　铜质
The 1900s, copper, 7.7 cm in opening diameter, 12 cm in bottom diameter, and 11 cm in height, Yunnan

烧水用具。带环形纽壶盖，敛口，鼓腹，平底，有两根粗铁丝做成的提梁。纽和提梁间有细铁环相系，避免壶盖丢失。

带盖提梁铜壶

Copper Kettle with Lid and Arc Handle

20 世纪　云南　口径 11.5 厘米　底径 21 厘米　高 26.5 厘米　铜质

The 1900s, copper, 11.5 cm in opening diameter, 21 cm in bottom diameter, and 26.5 cm in height, Yunnan

烧水用具。带环形纽壶盖，敛口，溜肩，鼓腹，平底，粗大的管状铜质提梁方便提拿。纽和提梁间以小铜环相连，避免壶盖丢失。

龙形柄刻花嵌瓷片陶执壶

Tile-inlaid Pottery Jug with Carved Pattern and Dragon-shaped Handle

20 世纪　云南　口径 9 厘米　底径 11.5 厘米　高 22 厘米　陶质

The 1900s, pottery, 9 cm in opening diameter, 11.5 cm in bottom diameter, and 22 cm in height, Yunnan

盛煮茶用具。盘口，溜肩，鼓腹，平底，上有类似弦纹状的数圈凸起和用瓷片粘贴出的图案和纹饰。

刻花嵌瓷片陶执壶

Tile-inlaid Pottery Jug with Carved Pattern

20 世纪　云南　口径 10 厘米　底径 8.7 厘米　高 20.5 厘米　陶质

The 1900s, pottery, 10 cm in opening diameter, 8.7 cm in bottom diameter, and 20.5 cm in height, Yunnan

盛煮茶用具。盘口，溜肩，鼓腹，平底，上有弦纹状的凸起和刻花，用瓷片粘贴出不同的图案和纹饰。

刻花陶执壶

Pottery Jug with Carved Pattern

20 世纪　云南　口径 9 厘米　底径 7.6 厘米　高 20 厘米　陶质

The 1900s, pottery, 9 cm in opening diameter, 7.6 cm in bottom diameter, and 20 cm in height, Yunnan

盛煮茶用具。盘口，溜肩，鼓腹，平底，雕刻圆圈、动植物等纹样。

6. 葫芦器　Gourd Vessels

葫芦器轻巧便于携带，是行走的马帮装水、盛酒最常用的器物。许多葫芦器只要简单地开口系绳就可以使用了。有的葫芦器外包竹编或皮条编成的外壳，方便挂在驮架上长途携带。

Gourd vessels are lightweight, easy to carry, and the caravan's commonest vessels for water or liquor. Most of them were simply made by making a hole in the gourd and attaching a string to it. Some go with bamboo or leather weaved case to make it easier to carry by hanging them from the pack rack.

葫芦器
Gourd Vessel

20 世纪　云南　口径 6 厘米　腹径 12 厘米　高 29 厘米　葫芦质
The 1900s, gourd, 6 cm in opening diameter, 12 cm in major diameter, and 29 cm in height, Yunnan

在葫芦的颈部和腹部连接处割开一个口子，就可以往里注入酒水，方便饮用。葫芦长颈上系绳，便于携带。

葫芦器

Gourd Vessel

20 世纪　云南　口径 8 厘米　腹径 20 厘米　高 33 厘米　绳长 25 厘米　葫芦质

The 1900s, gourd, 8 cm in opening diameter, 20 cm in major diameter, 33 cm in height, and 25 cm in string length, Yunnan

在葫芦的腹部挖一个圆口，注入酒水，方便饮用。葫芦长颈上穿孔系绳，便于携带。

葫芦器

Gourd Vessel

20 世纪　云南　口径 4 厘米　腹径 15 厘米　高 20 厘米　绳长 14 厘米　葫芦质

The 1900s, gourd, 4 cm in opening diameter, 15 cm in major diameter, 20 cm in height, and 14 cm in string length, Yunnan

短颈，深腹，在葫芦的颈部开一个圆口，注入酒水，方便饮用。在顶端系绳，方便携带。

葫芦器
Gourd Vessel

20 世纪　云南　口径 1.5 厘米　腹径 15 厘米　高 23 厘米　绳长 13 厘米　葫芦质

The 1900s, gourd, 1.5 cm in opening diameter, 15 cm in major diameter, 23 cm in height, and 13 cm in string length, Yunnan

双鼓腹，上小下大，顶端开口，注入酒水不易溢出，中间束腰处系麻绳，便于携带。

葫芦器
Gourd Vessel

20 世纪　云南　口径 1 厘米　腹径 14 厘米　高 22 厘米　葫芦质
The 1900s, gourd, 1 cm in opening diameter, 14 cm in major diameter and 22 cm in height, Yunnan

直口，溜肩，束腰，双鼓腹，上小下大，顶端开口，注入酒水不易溢出，中间束腰处系绳，便于携带。

葫芦器

Gourd Vessel

20 世纪　口径 3 厘米　腹径 12 厘米　高 25.5 厘米　葫芦质

The 1900s, gourd, 3 cm in opening diameter, 12 cm in major diameter and 25.5 cm in height

直口，溜肩，束腰，上小下大，上半部圆柱形腹，下半部球形腹，顶端开口，注入酒水不易溢出，顶端钻孔系绳，便于携带。

竹套葫芦器

Gourd Vessel with Bamboo Case

20 世纪　云南　口径 8 厘米　腹径 25 厘米　高 25 厘米　葫芦、竹质

The 1900s, gourd and bamboo, 8 cm in opening diameter, 25 cm in major diameter, and 25 cm in height, Yunnan

罐状，平口，短颈，深腹，外面有竹条做的竹套保护，竹套上方系有绳索，便于携带。

7. 烟具　Smoking Set

因为马帮长途跋涉的生活，枯燥又辛苦，所以赶马人会在休息时抽烟来解乏提神。马帮常用的烟具主要有旱烟斗、水烟筒和鼻烟壶等。吸水烟算是马帮汉子的抽烟“大餐”了，每到歇息的时候，马帮汉子最享受的就是吸水烟。水烟筒的材质一般为竹、木，也有金属材质的。2022 年暑期调研时，笔者在云南镇沅九甲镇和德钦奔子栏都见到了吸水烟的人。奔子栏吸水烟的藏族餐馆老板告诉笔者，他们那里的水烟筒是从傣族那里传过来的。傣族一般用竹质的烟筒，因奔子栏盛产木器，后来就改成木质的烟筒了。按他所说，水烟筒是这两个民族文化交流的物证。

鼻烟又称“闻烟”，据说起源于南美印第安人。它是将烟叶研磨成细末，掺入芳香类物质，并装入蜡丸中密封陈化数年制成的。其用法是直接涂抹在鼻孔内嗅吸。鼻烟含有珍贵药材，有提神醒脑、驱寒除湿、解除疲劳之功效。鼻烟壶通常镶嵌珊瑚、玛瑙、松石和其他宝石，雍容华贵、光彩夺目，是马锅头身份和财富的象征。

The caravan's long, arduous journey was tiring and boring, so the horse drivers would smoke while resting to recover from fatigue and refresh themselves. The common smoking sets include pipes, hookah, and snuff bottles. Smoking a hookah was a “feast” for the caravan men, and when it was the time for rest, hookah was their greatest pleasure. Hookah is usually made of bamboo, wood or metal. During the summer investigation in 2022, we saw some people smoking hookahs in Jiujia Village, Zhenyuan County and Benzilan Village, Deqin County, Yunnan. The owner of a Tibetan food restaurant in Benzilan, who smokes hookah, told us that they had learned to smoke it from the Dai people who generally use bamboo hookahs. Because Benzilan produced large quantities of wooden furniture, the hookah there was later made of wood instead of bamboo. According to what he said, the hookah is the real evidence of the interaction and blending between the two peoples.

Snuff, also called “smelling”, is said to have come from Indians in South America. It is made by grinding tobacco into powder, adding aromatic substances, and sealing it up in a round waxed case to age for years. It can be directly applied to the nostrils for sniffing and inhalation. Snuff containing precious medicinal herbs can lift one's spirit, take the chill and dampness off the body, and relieve fatigue. Snuff bottles are normally decorated with coral, agate, turquoise and other gems, looking dignified, graceful and dazzlingly brilliant, symbolizing the status and wealth of Maguotou.

竹水烟筒

Bamboo Hookah

20 世纪　云南　长 88.5 厘米　宽 12.7 厘米　高 23.5 厘米　竹质
The 1900s, bamboo, 88.5 cm × 12.7 cm × 23.5 cm, Yunnan

由竹筒简单制作而成。在下面一节靠近底部的地方，斜插进竹质的烟嘴，无装饰物。水烟筒里灌水，一般水深不超过烟嘴顶端。经过水过滤，不仅能过滤掉一些尼古丁，还能令烟气更加清凉醇和，抽了不易上火。

竹水烟筒

Bamboo Hookah

20 世纪　云南　长 75.4 厘米　宽 7.6 厘米　高 15 厘米　竹质
The 1900s, bamboo, 75.4 cm × 7.6 cm × 15 cm, Yunnan

烟嘴上有爪样装饰物。烟筒上刻有“忍一时风平浪静，让一步海阔天空”的字样。上半部还刻有竹子图案和“玉竹青芽，鸟语花香”的字样，中下半部刻有“君子兰”字样及兰花图案。梅、兰、竹、菊在中原文化中被誉为花中四君子。兰花代表豁达贤明的精神，竹子代表谦虚大气的潇洒品性。君子文化是中华民族独特的精神标识，君子人格是中国人独特的理想人格。以上这些图案和字样表达了赶马人对君子人格的推崇和欣赏，这也是民族交往、交流、交融的物证之一。

竹水烟筒
Bamboo Hookah

20 世纪　云南　长 63 厘米　宽 6.5 厘米　高 12.5 厘米　竹、铜、铝质
The 1900s, bamboo, brass and aluminum, 63 cm × 6.5 cm × 12.5 cm, Yunnan

由局部包铜皮和铝皮的竹筒制成，在下面一节靠近底部的地方，斜插进竹质的烟嘴。烟嘴上有铜皮包着的指尖状装饰物。包有铜、铝等金属材质的外壳起到保护和装饰的作用。

镶松石银鼻烟壶

Silver Snuff Bottle Inlaid with Turquoise

藏族 20 世纪 云南 长 9 厘米 宽 4 厘米 高 14 厘米 链长 12 厘米 银、石质

The 1900s, silver and turquoise, 9 cm × 4 cm × 14 cm, 12 cm in chain length, Tibetan, Yunnan

扁壶形，平口，带盖，壶身呈喇叭形。盖上有镶红宝石的纽，由一条银链和肩部凸起的圆环相连，避免盖丢失。腹部中间和肩部镶嵌绿松石，藏传佛教双鱼吉祥图案围绕腹部中间的绿松石，象征着复苏、永生和再生。

镶宝石葫芦形铜鼻烟壶

Gourd-shaped Brass Snuff Bottle Inlaid with Gems

藏族　20 世纪　云南　长 6 厘米　宽 5 厘米　高 12 厘米　铜、石质

The 1900s, brass and gem, 6 cm × 5 cm × 12 cm, Tibetan, Yunnan

葫芦状，平口，带盖，金色的金属丝内嵌满大小不一的红、绿料石珠和绿松石，色彩斑斓、富丽华贵，彰显主人的财富和地位。

镶宝石方形铜鼻烟壶

Square Brass Snuff Bottle Inlaid with Gems

藏族　20 世纪　云南　长 6 厘米　宽 3 厘米　高 10 厘米　铜、石质

The 1900s, brass and gem, 6 cm × 3 cm × 10 cm, Tibetan, Yunnan

扁瓶形，平口，带盖，在金色的金属丝内镶嵌大小均匀的红料石珠和规格不一的绿松石。腹部中间的绿松石为长方形，其余的为小珠状。鼻烟壶上可系绳，便于携带。

8. 火镰　Steel for Flint

火镰，也叫作火刀，通常为铁质，藏式的火镰通常有铜钉、红珊瑚、绿松石等装饰，是茶马古道上最古老的取火器物。火镰一般由火石、火绒和钢条三部分组成。火石学名燧石，受到碰撞时会产生火星。火绒是艾蒿的嫩叶。钢条常打造成镰刀的形状，便于碰撞火石，产生火星后点燃易燃的火绒。马帮在野外宿营，不仅需要生火做饭，也需要用明火驱赶夜间的野兽。

Steel for flint is also called sickle for fire, usually made of iron, and a Tibetan steel for flint is decorated with brass studs, red coral and turquoise, which is the oldest tool for starting a fire on the Ancient Tea-Horse Road. The steel for flint generally consists of three elements—fire stone, tinder and steel bar. The fire stone, formally called flint, can produce a spark when hit against steel. The tinder is made of tender leaves of mugwort. The steel bar was often made into the shape of a sickle to facilitate its strike against the flint so that sparks are produced to ignite the tinder. When camping out, the caravan not only needed to make a fire to cook, but also to repel the wild beasts.

铜钉皮套铁火镰
Steel for Flint with Brass Nails and Leather Sleeves

藏族　20 世纪　云南　长 15 厘米　宽 2 厘米　高 10 厘米　皮、铜、铁、松石质
The 1900s, leather, brass, iron and turquoise, 15 cm × 2 cm × 10 cm, Tibetan, Yunnan

火镰内为钢条，外面皮套上镶嵌铜钉和松石，一侧顶端有环形纽，便于穿绳携带。

铜钉皮套铁火镰

Steel for Flint with Brass Nails and Leather Sleeves

20 世纪　云南　长 14 厘米　宽 3 厘米　高 8 厘米　皮、铜、铁质

The 1900s, leather, brass and iron, 14 cm × 3 cm × 8 cm, Yunnan

火镰外面有红棕色的皮质套，镶嵌铜钉和金属装饰物，一侧顶端系有皮绳，方便携带。

铜钉皮套铁火镰

Steel for Flint with Brass Nails and Leather Sleeves

20 世纪　云南　长 13 厘米　宽 1 厘米　高 7 厘米　皮、铜、铁质

The 1900s, leather, brass and iron, 13 cm × 1 cm × 7 cm, Yunnan

火镰外面有棕色的小皮质套，使钢条大部分外露，一面镶嵌铜钉装饰，另一面有铁片装饰和环形纽，上系绳，方便携带。

（三）住 Accommodations

马帮穿行于山水之间，通道上便产生了许多驿站，其中的马店就是马帮住宿歇脚的地方，他们在这里享受一下难得的床铺。除马锅头因其身份和携带贵重东西而单独住一间房外，其余赶马人睡觉的地方多为类似北方地区的大炕，普洱地区称为大懒敞铺，中原地区称为大通铺。大懒敞铺方便大家聊天、喝茶、唱歌。马店一般设在驿道旁的镇边村角不太拥挤也不过分偏僻之处，方便进出，也便于马帮寻认和购买草料及生活用物。

马店要帮着照料牲口，看守驮子，第二天清晨赶马人要上路时，马店里的人要帮着上驮子。有些马店，没有规定好食宿费，离开时，凭良心给上一点食宿费，店家要客气一番才肯收下。每年春节前后来住店的，只要马锅头说这是今年最后一趟马帮了，有的店家除了免收草料钱，还好菜好饭招待，这叫“扫店饭”。在迄今犹存的百年马店那柯里“荣发马店”的门楣上，有一副对联，上联是

普洱忠义驿站博物馆里的大懒敞铺

"关山难越谁为主"，下联为"萍水相逢我做东"。这份豪迈与侠情令人赞叹！藏族的马帮一般不住店，是在城郊开亮（露宿）。

馆藏的马店用品有牌匾、灯具、床具、家具、喂马工具和饲料以及日用品等，其中马灯、鼓风机和饲料等在路上也要使用。

The caravan travelled among mountains and rivers. As a result, many daks appeared along the road, and one of them was caravansary in which the caravan would stay for the night and have a rest, enjoying a rare bed on the way. Maguotou could have a single room to himself because of his position and valuables on him, and the others in the caravan had to sleep on what is similar to the "big kang" (a big brick or earth brick bed) in the North of China. However, the kang made it easy for them to chat, drink tea and sing. The caravansary was usually located on the outskirts of a town or a village by which a post road passed, which was neither too crowed nor too remote, and convenient to come in and go out, find, get forages and daily necessities.

The staff of a caravansary should look after the caravans' pack animals, watch over the goods, and help loading the goods when the caravan was leaving. Some caravansaries had no fixed prices for accommodations, so the going caravan would offer some money for the costs with a conscience, and the proprietor would take it only after some words of courtesy. Around the Spring Festival, as long as Maguotou said that it was the last business trip of the year for his caravan, some caravansaries would not only provide free forages but also treat them to good meals called "last meal of the year". On the door posts of "Rongfa", an extant century-old caravansary in Nakeli, there is a couplet reading "I can come to your help if in trouble; I stand treat though we meet by chance." What knightliness and generosity! The Tibetan caravans did not stay in a caravansary but camp out on the outskirts of a town.

The museum collection about the caravansary includes plaques, lighting devices, bed and bedding, furniture, tools for feeding horses and forages and daily necessities, among which horse lamps, bellows and forages were also used on the way.

1. 马店牌匾　Caravansaries' Plaques

蒙化（巍山）因地处要冲，南来北往，马帮云集，人气很旺。不足万人的小城镇，曾有大小马店 20 余家，如蒙记马店、重兴店、合义老店、兴隆店、茶升店、百宝生、唐记老客栈、李记世生马店等，这些店基本是在古城北门外（拱辰楼）日升、月华两街上。此外，还有许多鸡毛店，数不胜数。其中始于清末、历史逾百年的李记世生马店至今仍在，第五代掌店人米德润大妈经营祖传马店 40 余年，亲历马帮时代的沧桑变化，堪称这座滇西南小城的一个传奇。

百年李记世生马店

Menghua (Weishan) was a communication hub, so caravans on the way would stop there for a rest. In this small town of less than ten thousand people, there used to be 20 caravansaries, big or small, like Meng's, Chongxing, Heyi, Xinglong, Chasheng, Baibaosheng, Tang's, Lijishisheng, which were almost located on the two streets—Risheng and Yuehua—outside the north gate of the old town. Moreover, there were countless simple inns. Of all the caravansaries mentioned above, Lijishisheng, starting in the late Qing dynasty, has been run by its fifth generation proprietor Auntie Miderun for over 40 years, who has witnessed the changes of the caravan time and is seen as a legend in the little town of western Yunnan.

蒙记马店牌匾
Meng's Plaque

20 世纪　云南　长 107 厘米　厚 4.2 厘米　高 36.7 厘米　木质
The 1900s, wood, 107 cm × 4.2 cm × 36.7 cm, Yunnan

长方形木板，表面以黑漆为底，先雕刻出匾文，红漆勾勒填写。经风吹日晒，黑漆已基本脱落，颜色斑驳的牌匾上布满了虫眼，显露出岁月的痕迹。

茶升店牌匾
Chasheng's Plaque

20 世纪　云南　长 93 厘米　厚 6 厘米　高 36.3 厘米　木质
The 1900s, wood, 93 cm × 6 cm × 36.3 cm, Yunnan

长方形木板，表面以红漆为底，先雕刻出匾文，再用金粉描字，后面接皮绳，便于悬挂固定。

兴隆店牌匾
Xinglong's Plaque

20 世纪　云南　长 110 厘米　厚 4.3 厘米　高 37 厘米　木质
The 1900s, wood, 110 cm × 4.3 cm × 37 cm, Yunnan

长方形木板，表面以黑漆为底，先雕刻出匾文，再用金粉描字，后面系皮绳，便于悬挂固定。

重兴店牌匾

Chongxing's Plaque

20 世纪　云南　长 104 厘米　厚 5 厘米　高 42 厘米　木质

The 1900s, wood, 104 cm × 5 cm × 42 cm, Yunnan

长方形木板，表面刷漆，先雕刻出匾文，再用金粉描字，底漆基本脱落，露出原色，后面系尼龙绳，用于悬挂固定。

合义店牌匾
Heyi's Plaque

20 世纪　云南　长 117 厘米　厚 4 厘米　高 45.2 厘米　木质
The 1900s, wood, 117 cm × 4 cm × 45.2 cm, Yunnan

长方形木板，表面以黑漆为底，先雕刻出匾文，再用金粉描字，底漆部分脱落，两边各有两个凹陷，后面系麻绳，用于悬挂固定。

2. 灯具　Lighting Devices

油灯是茶马古道上最古老的照明工具，材质有陶瓷、竹、玻璃、金属等，燃料使用豆油、酥油、橄榄油等。灯捻子是多孔的植物纤维灯芯，能够吸油且燃烧慢。馆藏的瓷油灯简易省油，竹节马灯用竹子全手工制作，为带提梁的照明油灯。20 世纪中期上海光华桅灯厂和天津市制灯厂等生产的燃煤油的桅灯，本是挂在船桅杆上用的，但桅灯带提梁，其供油系统非常科学，四两油可以持续燃烧 12 个小时，夜行时可挂在马身上，实用且携带方便，就成了行走的马帮最常用的灯具，人们称之为"马灯"。马灯在滇、川、藏区的广泛使用，与马帮在这些地区行走密切相关。

Oil lamps were the oldest lighting devices on the Ancient Tea-Horse Road, made of such materials as porcelain, bamboo, glass or metal, using lamp fuels like soy bean oil, ghee, olive oil, etc. The wick was made from porous plant fiber and capable of absorbing oil and burning slowly. The ceramic oil lamp in the collection is simple and fuel-efficient, and the bamboo horse lamp has an arc handle, all hand-made with bamboo. In the mid-1900s, Shanghai Guanghua Mast Light Factory and Tianjin Lighting Factory produced kerosene mast lights designed for ship masts. But they had arc handles, and with their well-designed fuel supply system, 200 grams of oil could keep burning 12 hours, and they could be hung from the horse at night on the way, thus the most commonly used lighting devices for the caravan and named "horse lamp". They were widely used in Yunnan, Sichuan and Tibet, which attribute much to the caravans' travel there.

褐彩瓷油灯
Brown-colored Porcelain Oil Lamp

20 世纪　云南　口径 6 厘米　底径 7.3 厘米　高 15 厘米　瓷质
The 1900s, porcelain, 6 cm in opening diameter, 7.3 cm in bottom diameter and 15 cm in height, Yunnan

顶端撇口，束颈，腹鼓起后渐收成柱形，平底，下接喇叭状高圈足。此油灯内部深，一贯到底，下部可盛水，仅在上部盛油和放置灯芯捻子，这样可节省油量。

褐彩瓷油灯

Brown-colored Porcelain Oil Lamp

20 世纪　云南　口径 5.5 厘米　底径 7.9 厘米　高 16.4 厘米　瓷质

The 1900s, porcelain, 5.5 cm in opening diameter, 7.9 cm in bottom diameter, 16.4 cm in height, Yunnan

顶端撇口，束颈，腹鼓起后渐收成柱形，碗状底部下接喇叭状高圈足。此油灯内部一贯到底，可节省油量。在中间碗状处，放油和灯芯捻子，可以点亮第二盏灯增加亮度。

竹节马灯
Bamboo Joint Horse Lamp

20 世纪前期　云南　长 14 厘米　宽 15 厘米　高 35 厘米　竹质
The early-1900s, bamboo, 14 cm × 15 cm × 35 cm, Yunnan

竹节马灯是茶马古道上最简单和方便的灯具。竹筒做盛油的容器，放置在由竹条搭起的架子上面，架子的上面接一个用宽竹片弯曲制成的提梁，便于携带。

竹节马灯

Bamboo Joint Horse Lamp

20 世纪前期　云南　长 12.5 厘米　宽 13 厘米　高 32 厘米　竹质

The early-1900s, bamboo, 12.5 cm × 13 cm × 32 cm, Yunnan

竹筒做盛油的容器，其边缘有一个方便放灯芯的缺口，将其放置在由竹条搭起的架子上面，架子的上面接一个底部用双层细竹片弯曲制成的提梁，便于携带。

玻璃煤油灯

Glass Kerosene Lamp

20 世纪前中期　云南　口径 6 厘米　底径 10 厘米　高 15.5 厘米　玻璃、铁质

The early and mid-1900s, glass and iron, 6 cm in opening diameter, 10 cm in bottom diameter, and 15.5 cm in height, Yunnan

上海华民玻璃厂生产的灯具。玻璃瓶为盛煤油的容器，喇叭形圈足，顶端有一圈水滴状凸起，中间刻有 4 只鸣叫的公鸡图案。玻璃容器上接的铁质部分，一侧圆形纽可调灯的亮度，中间小管放灯芯捻子，外侧 4 个铁片是支撑已遗失的玻璃灯罩的，防止风吹灭灯，底座刻有“上海华民玻璃厂出品”的字样。

玻璃煤油灯

Glass Kerosene Lamp

20 世纪前中期　云南　口径 6 厘米　底径 8 厘米　高 18.5 厘米　玻璃、铁质

The early and mid-1900s, glass and iron, 6 cm in opening diameter, 8 cm in bottom diameter, and 18.5 cm in height, Yunnan

玻璃瓶为盛煤油的容器，喇叭形圈足，玻璃容器上接的铁质部分，一侧圆形钮可调灯的亮度，中间小管里有灯芯捻子，外侧 4 个铁片是支撑已遗失的玻璃灯罩的，防止风吹灭灯。

蓝色铁马灯

Blue Iron Horse Lamp

20 世纪中期　云南　长 15 厘米　宽 11.5 厘米　高 25 厘米　玻璃、铁质

The mid-1900s, glass and iron, 15 cm × 11.5 cm × 25 cm, Yunnan

上海光华桅灯厂生产的 235 规格灯具。底座为油壶，上有带盖的小口，用来添加煤油。扁条状的灯芯外罩玻璃罩。玻璃罩外有铁丝、把状的保护物。铁丝为提梁，便于携带。其顶端有“中国上海”及其英文翻译“SHANGHAI.CHINA”的字样，底座一侧有“光华”及“235”的字样，另一侧有“KANG HWA.WARN—USE ONLY PARAFFIN”（译为“光华，提醒——仅用于煤油”）字样。

铁马灯

Iron Horse Lamp

20 世纪中期　云南　长 18 厘米　宽 14 厘米　高 29 厘米　玻璃、铁质

The mid-1900s, glass and iron, 18 cm × 14 cm × 29 cm, Yunnan

上海光华桅灯厂生产的 225 规格的灯具。其顶端有“中国上海”及其英文翻译“SHANGHAI.CHINA”的字样，底座一侧有“光华”及“225”的字样，另一侧有“KANG HWA.WARN—USE ONLY PARAFFIN”（译为“光华，提醒——仅用于煤油”）字样。

铁马灯
Iron Horse Lamp

20 世纪中期　云南　长 17 厘米　宽 14.4 厘米　高 29 厘米　玻璃、铁质
The mid-1900s, glass and iron, 17 cm × 14.4 cm × 29 cm, Yunnan

天津市制灯厂生产的永明牌 203 规格的灯具。底座上有“中国天津 203”的字样。当时生产的这种灯具有 202、203、205、206、208、647 等多种不同的规格，不同的规格盛煤油量不同，这种 203 规格的盛油量为 250 克。

竹套铁皮洋油桶

Iron Sheet Coal Oil Bucket with Bamboo Case

20 世纪　云南　长 29.5 厘米　宽 29 厘米　高 37 厘米　竹、铁质

The 1900s, iron and bamboo, 29.5 cm × 29 cm × 37 cm, Yunnan

装煤油用具。里面由铁皮制成，外面有竹编的保护套，顶端有环形纽，便于系绳提拿和固定。洋油指煤油，主要用于照明的煤油是 19 世纪下半叶从国外引进的，故称其为“洋油”。中国沿海和内陆的城市、乡村皆用它来点灯。

3. 床具和家具　Bedding and Furniture

馆藏马店的床不高，但简单结实。实木床板上铺一层草席，摆放着用棉布包裹的棉花或荞麦壳的枕头。这种简陋的住宿条件对常年露宿的赶马人来说也是难得的舒适环境。除了床具之外，馆藏的马店家具还有四方桌、两头沉的桌子等。

The bed in a caravansary in the collection was low, but simple and durable. Its board was covered with a straw mat, equipped with a cotton or buckwheat husk pillow with a cotton fabric case. The simple accommodation was rarely comfortable for the horse driver who often camped out. Bedding apart, the collection includes a square table, a double pedestal desk, etc.

红漆木床
Red Lacquer Wooden Bed

20 世纪　云南　长 186 厘米　宽 110 厘米　高 53 厘米　木质
The 1900s, wood, 186 cm × 110 cm × 53 cm, Yunnan

纯实木制成，表面刷红漆，床框正中底部有对称、大小不一的弧形纹样，四足削尖和床体连接，上有简洁的对称装饰纹样，简单之中不乏美感。

木床
Wooden Bed

20 世纪　云南　长 195 厘米　宽 102 厘米　高 53 厘米　木质
The 1900s, wood, 195 cm × 102 cm × 53 cm, Yunnan

纯实木制成，床框正中底部有对称、大小不一的弧形纹样，四足削尖和床体连接，有对称的装饰纹样。

草席
Straw Mat

20 世纪　云南　长 240 厘米　宽 89 厘米　高 4 厘米　草质
The 1900s, straw, 240 cm × 89 cm × 4 cm, Yunnan

草束编织而成，边缘编织成辫状锁边，内以草束间隔均匀，系绳后和相邻的草束交叉编织而成，这样既蓬松又整齐。

草席
Straw Mat

20 世纪　云南　长 200 厘米　宽 83 厘米　草质
The 1900s, straw, 200 cm × 83 cm, Yunnan

用稻草平织而成，两边以线锁边。

“卍”字纹枕头

Pillow with Swastika Pattern

20 世纪 云南 长 40 厘米 宽 20 厘米 高 12 厘米 布、棉花质

The 1900s, fabric and cotton, 40 cm × 20 cm × 12 cm, Yunnan

长方形，里面装棉花，中间表面以黑布分层包裹，两端用红、白布拼接包裹，两侧枕顶为 4 个“卍”字吉祥图案，均为手工缝制。“卍”字纹寓意万福万寿、绵长不断。

打籽绣花草纹枕头

Pillow with Knot-stitched Floral Design

20 世纪　云南　长 70 厘米　宽 14 厘米　高 13 厘米　布、荞麦壳质

The 1900s, fabric and buckwheat husk, 70 cm × 14 cm × 13 cm, Yunnan

长方形，里面装荞麦壳，外面简单以白布包裹，现已不易看出原色，局部因破损而打上补丁。两侧枕顶有手工缝制的打籽绣花草纹饰。

四方形木桌
Square Wooden Table

20 世纪　云南　长 101 厘米　宽 94 厘米　高 63 厘米　木质
The 1900s, wood, 101 cm × 94 cm × 63 cm, Yunnan

近似正方形，桌面朴素无纹，由两块木板拼接而成，四周边框上方雕刻花朵纹和回纹装饰，下方则有对称的波浪纹装饰。

黑红漆两头沉木桌

Blackish Red Lacquer Double Pedestal Desk

20 世纪　云南　长 103 厘米　宽 41 厘米　高 86 厘米　木质

The 1900s, wood, 103 cm × 41 cm × 86 cm, Yunnan

用黑红两色漆装饰，桌面平素无纹，正面中间雕刻对称的波浪纹，两个抽屉的把手为八瓣花状的小瓷饼，精美别致。

4. 日用品　Necessities

马店有许多日用品，馆藏的有马帮挑运货物的木扁担、算账用的算盘、量粮食的斤搭、木工活用具墨斗、取暖的石火盆、助燃的风筒和驱蚊的拂尘等。

There were a lot of daily necessities in a caravansary and the museum collection includes wooden shoulder poles for carrying a load, an abacus for counting or doing calculations, a Jinda for measuring grain, a carpenter's ink marker for woodworking, a stone brazier for giving warmth, a bellows for making a fire burn better and a duster to repel mosquitoes.

尖头兽蹄木扁担
Pointed-end Wooden Shoulder Pole with Animal Hoof Decoration

20 世纪　云南　长 166 厘米　宽 11 厘米　高 9.3 厘米　木质
The 1900s, wood, 166 cm × 11 cm × 9.3 cm, Yunnan

两端尖头，搬运货物时，不仅方便插入货物，可抬可挑，有时候还可当防身的武器。在扁担的一侧套有兽蹄做成的装饰物，可防止所负担的驮包滑动。

铁角尖头兽蹄木扁担
Wooden Shoulder Pole with Iron-capped Pointed Ends and Animal Hoof Decoration

20 世纪　云南　长 147.8 厘米　宽 8 厘米　高 5.5 厘米　木、铁质
The 1900s, wood and iron, 147.8 cm × 8 cm × 5.5 cm, Yunnan

尖头两端包铁角，既可以保护木质的尖头不易受损、经久耐用，也不会增加太大的负担。在扁担的一侧也套有已缺损的兽蹄做成的装饰物来防止驮包滑动。

木算盘
Wooden Abacus

20 世纪　云南　长 28.5 厘米　宽 14.5 厘米　高 2 厘米　木、铁质
The 1900s, wood and iron, 28.5 cm × 14.5 cm × 2 cm, Yunnan

算盘左右两边对称的第四根穿珠柱子的材质为铁质，其余的均为木质。部分接口处包铁皮来加固保护。

牛角墨斗
Ox Horn Carpenter's Ink Marker

20 世纪　云南　长 28 厘米　宽 11 厘米　高 10 厘米　牛角质
The 1900s, ox horn, 28 cm × 11 cm × 10 cm, Yunnan

传统木工常用的工具。一般由墨仓、线轮、墨线（包括线锥）、墨签四部分构成。墨斗多为木质的，牛角制成的较为少见。

木斤搭

Wooden Jinda

20 世纪　云南　长 38 厘米　宽 38 厘米　高 22 厘米　木质

The 1900s, wood, 38 cm × 38 cm × 22 cm, Yunnan

米面等粮食商品交易时的计量用具。敞口平底，中间有方便手提的横梁，边缘有一缺口。一搭为一市斤。

石火盆
Stone Brazier

20 世纪　云南　长 42 厘米　宽 37 厘米　高 14 厘米　石质
The 1900s, stone, 42 cm × 37 cm × 14 cm, Yunnan

烤火用具。将一块石材中间挖凿出圆洞做成火盆取暖。石火盆安全，只是不易挪动位置。4 个短足使石火盆显得不那么沉重。

圆形木风筒
Tube-shaped Wooden Bellows

20 世纪　云南　长 21 厘米　宽 7.5 厘米　高 73 厘米　木质
The 1900s, wood, 21 cm × 7.5 cm × 73 cm, Yunnan

鼓风吹火工具。里面中空带活塞，底部衔接一根木条用于稳定，外接一个手拉把，依靠一上一下的抽拉，把风抽进来送到助燃点助燃。除了马店会用到风筒外，马帮风餐露宿，有时遇雨雪，火燃不起来，也需要用这种工具。

牦牛尾拂尘

Yak Tail Duster

20 世纪　云南　长 77 厘米　宽 35 厘米　高 4 厘米　毛质

The 1900s, yak tail, 77 cm × 35 cm × 4 cm, Yunnan

除尘或驱赶蚊蝇用具。拂尘，又称尘拂、拂子、尘尾，用牦牛尾制成。顶端有铁丝做成的挂钩方便悬挂。马帮在外露宿时也会用到。

5. 喂马工具和饲料　Tools for Feeding Horses and Forage

马店里喂马工具是必不可少的。馆藏喂马工具有碎草料的铡刀，装盛马料的木桶、木盆、木槽、木勺和给骡马喂药的牛角灌勺等。在马的喂养方面，豆渣饼是常用的给马提供营养和补充能量的饲料。马帮中还有“不识中草药，枉为赶马人；不能治马病，不算赶马人”之说。据他们的经验，可给腹部鼓胀、大便不通的马喂香油润肠，给肠痛病的马灌竹烟筒水等。

Tools for feeding horses were absolutely necessary in a caravansary. The museum collection includes fodder choppers for cutting straw or hay, wooden buckets for holding fodder, wooden basins, wooden troughs, wooden scoops and ox horn drug feeders for feeding medicine. In addition to straw or hay, soya cake was often used to provide nutrient and energy. Among the caravan, a saying went that “whoever doesn't know Chinese medicinal herbs is not much of a horse driver; whoever can't treat a horse is not much of a horse driver.” From experience, they fed sesame oil to the bloated or constipated horse, and fed water from bamboo hookah to the horse with an intestinal pain.

木马槽

Wooden Trough

20 世纪　云南　长 123 厘米　宽 52 厘米　高 43 厘米　木质

The 1900s, wood, 123 cm × 52 cm × 43 cm, Yunnan

盛马食用具。由一根整木劈开后刳空而成。一侧有些向内凹陷，两端已有裂口。

木套铁铡刀

Iron Fodder Chopper with Wooden Case

藏族　20 世纪　云南　长 59 厘米　宽 8 厘米　高 3 厘米　木、铁质

The 1900s, wood and iron, 59 cm × 8 cm × 3 cm, Tibetan, Yunnan

碎草用具。铡刀由木质的刀把、刀柄和铁质的刀身组成，顶端有凸起的棍状物，其头部扁平，可用于搅拌草料。

直柄木勺

Wooden Scoop with Straight Handle

20 世纪　云南　长 25 厘米　宽 12 厘米　高 7 厘米　木质

The 1900s, wood, 25 cm × 12 cm × 7 cm, Yunnan

盛马汤食用具。由直手柄和半圆形勺两部分组成，局部已有缺损。

牛角灌勺
Ox Horn Drug Feeder

20 世纪　云南　长 27 厘米　宽 7 厘米　高 7.5 厘米　牛角质
The 1900s, ox horn, 27 cm × 7 cm × 7.5 cm, Yunnan

给骡马灌药用具。一端口宽，另一端口窄，如漏斗一样。若遇马匹生病，赶马人将马头仰起，将牛角灌具的窄口端往马嘴里一塞，可迅速把配制好的汤药从宽口端灌入马腹中。窄口处系一红绳便于携带。

牛角灌勺
Ox Horn Drug Feeder

20 世纪　云南　长 37 厘米　宽 6.5 厘米　高 4 厘米　牛角质
The 1900s, ox horn, 37 cm × 6.5 cm × 4 cm, Yunnan

带盖木桶

Wooden Bucket with Lid

20 世纪　云南　长 43.5 厘米　宽 29 厘米　高 46.3 厘米　木质
The 1900s, wood, 43.5 cm × 29 cm × 46.3 cm, Yunnan

盛马汤食用具。两端有耳，便于手拿，桶身用竹条箍牢，盖子中间嵌一根木条，便于掀盖。底部有破损。高原气候寒冷，需要喂马温热的汤食，用这种带盖的木桶盛装汤食可保温，保证马健康强壮，这样马儿才能扛得住长途跋涉的艰辛，负重前行。

椭圆形木桶

Oval Wooden Bucket

20 世纪　云南　长 61 厘米　宽 45 厘米　高 51 厘米　木质

The 1900s, wood, 61 cm × 45 cm × 51 cm, Yunnan

盛马汤食用具。敞口平底，由木片拼接而成，桶身用竹条和铁丝箍牢，口沿有一处缺口，方便倒出食物。

豆渣饼
Soya Cake

20 世纪　云南　直径 31.5 厘米　高 31 厘米　豆质
The 1900s, soy bean, 31.5 cm in diameter and 31 cm in height, Yunnan

俗称“油菇”，是榨豆油后用油渣做的豆渣饼。通常十个为一捆，便于携带。赶马人将豆渣饼打碎后，按一定比例拌上红糖喂驮马，可以为驮马提供足够的蛋白质和营养物，补充能量。

四、护身用具 Self-protection Tools

马帮驮着货物长途跋涉，土匪、强盗还有猛兽是赶马人行走在路上最大的威胁。因此刀、火枪、铲、叉、矛和火药等是他们必备的防身用具。其中火药枪还可以用来狩猎以改善马帮的生活，在茶马古道，枪和火药不能分离，需要随身携带。此外，云南马帮还用一种特殊的方法来驱赶野兽，就是燃烧草果，其发出的气味辛辣难闻，虎狼也避之惟恐不及。

During the caravan's long, arduous journey for carrying goods, bandits, brigands or wild beasts were a great threat to the horse drivers on the way. Therefore, knives, muskets, tridents, shovels, spears and gunpowder were indispensable tools for self-protection. The muskets could also be used for hunting to treat themselves, and when they traveled along the Ancient Tea-Horse Road, muskets and gunpowder were inseparable and should be carried along. Besides, the Yunnan caravans used a special way to repel wild beasts, that's burning tsaoko amomum fruit, which gave such a nasty, pungent smell that tigers or wolves would shun it.

1. 刀具 Knives

刀是赶马人必备的防身工具，种类很多。刀鞘一般有两层，外为金属质，内为木质，方便贴合刀身。馆藏藏族马帮使用的刀具，通常雕刻精美的图案，内容多为龙、凤、鹿、虎等中国传统吉祥动物图案以及藏传佛教八宝图案等，蕴涵吉祥和护佑之意，呈现出各民族共享中华文化符号的事实。此外，茶马古道上常见的刀具还有阿昌族制作的户撒刀，藏族马帮也使用它。户撒刀工艺独特，质地精良，锋利耐用，有“柔可绕指，削铁如泥”之誉，久享盛名。

Knives of various kinds were must-have self-protection tools for the horse driver. The sheath usually has two layers—outer metal and inner wooden that fits well in with the blade. The Tibetan caravan's knives in the collection usually go with exquisitely carved traditional patterns mainly of dragon, phoenix, deer or tiger and of the Eight Treasure in Tibetan Buddhism, a symbol of auspiciousness and bless, showing the fact of various peoples sharing the same Chinese cultural symbols. Moreover, Husha knives from the Achang people in Yunnan were also common on the road, and used by the Tibetan caravan. Made exquisitely with unique process, sharp and durable, they have long enjoyed a good reputation that “they are so soft that they could turn around the finger; they are so sharp that they could an iron bar easily”.

八宝龙纹鞘钢刀

Steel Knife with Sheath of Eight Treasures and Dragon

20 世纪　云南　长 73 厘米　宽 9.2 厘米　高 4.7 厘米　钢铁、木质

The 1900s, steel and wood, 73 cm × 9.2 cm × 4.7 cm, Yunnan

刀把顶端一面雕刻莲花纹，另一面为龙头纹。刀鞘红丝绒为底，一面雕刻二龙戏珠吉祥图案，有庆丰年、祈吉祥之寓意；另一面雕刻八宝吉祥图案和花草纹。鞘尖上有弧形装饰物。

龙鹿纹鞘钢刀

Steel Knife with Sheath of Dragon and Deer

20 世纪　云南　长 55.3 厘米　宽 6 厘米　高 3 厘米　钢铁、木质

The 1900s, steel and wood, 55.3 cm × 6 cm × 3 cm, Yunnan

刀把顶端一面雕刻花朵纹。刀鞘一面雕刻龙纹和鹿纹，另一面雕刻花草纹。

龙纹鞘钢刀

Steel Knife with Sheath of Dragon

20世纪　云南　长54厘米　宽5.5厘米　高3厘米　钢铁、木质

The 1900s, steel and wood, 54 cm × 5.5 cm × 3 cm, Yunnan

刀把顶端雕刻聚宝、叶纹。刀鞘一面雕刻带须的龙纹、莲瓣和四叶草纹（四叶草在藏传佛教中寓意吉祥、幸福和成功），另一面无纹饰，上方焊有金属质的挂襻，连有皮绳便于悬挂和携带。

八宝纹鞘钢刀

Steel Knife with Sheath of Eight Treasures

20 世纪　云南　长 28 厘米　宽 5 厘米　高 3 厘米　钢铁、木质

The 1900s, steel and wood, 28 cm × 5 cm × 3 cm, Yunnan

刀鞘和刀把底为红色丝绒，表面镂空雕刻藏传佛教“轮螺伞盖花罐鱼长”八宝吉祥图案，侧面有铁丝状的挂襻便于携带，两端有明显的弧形装饰物。刀身较厚且锋利。

龙凤纹鞘钢刀

Steel Knife with Sheath of Dragon and Phoenix

20 世纪　云南　长 40 厘米　宽 6 厘米　高 3 厘米　钢铁、木质

The 1900s, steel and wood, 40 cm × 6 cm × 3 cm, Yunnan

刀鞘一面雕刻龙纹，另一面为花草纹。刀把顶端雕刻凤纹，与龙纹相对应。刀柄手持处有紧密缠绕的铁丝，方便把持。

龙凤纹鞘钢刀

Steel Knife with Sheath of Dragon an Phoenix

20 世纪　云南　长 22 厘米　宽 4 厘米　高 2 厘米　钢铁、木质

the 1900s, steel and wood, 22 cm × 4 cm × 2 cm, Yunnan

刀鞘一面刻有两眼突出的龙纹，另一面光滑无纹。刀把一面雕刻的变形凤纹飞舞与龙纹相对。手持处的铁丝缠绕紧密，便于手持。

龙凤纹鞘户撒钢刀

Husa Knife with Sheath of Dragon and Phoenix

20 世纪　云南　长 26 厘米　宽 4 厘米　高 2 厘米　钢铁、木质

The 1900s, steel and wood, 26 cm × 4 cm × 2 cm, Yunnan

刀把一面刻有虎纹。刀鞘一面刻有龙凤纹，带须的四爪龙纹，两眼和鼻子突出，身边祥云围绕，凤飞舞与之相对。龙凤纹之间刻有“户撒”和“龙飞凤舞”六个字。刀身轻薄锋利。

龙凤纹鞘户撒钢刀

Husa Knife with Sheath of Dragon and Phoenix

20 世纪　云南　长 20 厘米　宽 3 厘米　高 1.5 厘米　钢铁、木质

The 1900s, steel and wood, 20 cm × 3 cm × 1.5 cm, Yunnan

刀鞘刻有两眼突出的龙纹，身边祥云围绕。刀把雕刻凤纹飞舞与之相对。手持处有紧密缠绕的铁丝，下方刻有“户撒”两字。

2. 火枪 Muskets

火枪俗称钢炮枪，是马帮在途中防身和打猎的武器之一。这种枪大多由自己组装，结构简单，外形粗糙，有的仅用于打弹丸和沙子驱赶野兽。我国最早的火枪出现在南宋高宗时期，守将陈规将火药装进长竹竿制成了可以喷射火焰的火枪。后发展为用火绳点火的火绳枪，但一遇到风雨天气，火药不是被风吹走就是被雨浇灭。于是，明代的火器研究家毕懋康将火绳点火装置继续改进为利用燧石枪机点火发射。他发明的撞击式燧发枪只需扣扳机将龙头下压，就能利用弹簧的作用与火石摩擦发火，这样，不但克服了风雨天气对火绳枪射击所造成的困难，也大幅度地提高了发射速度和精确度。

The musket was one of the caravan's weapons for self-protection and hunting on their way. For the most part, the musket was roughly hand-made and simply structured, and some of them only fired pellets and grits to repel wild beasts. The earliest musket in China was made during the reign of Zhao Gou, an emperor in the Southern Song dynasty, when the garrison General Chen Gui first made it by putting explosive into a long bamboo pole to throw out fire, and later evolved into a matchlock with a trigger mechanism that ignited the powder with a slow-burning fuse. But in the event of wind or rain, the powder would be blown away or quenched. Then, Bi Maokang, a firearm expert in the Ming dynasty, used a flintlock instead of the matchlock. The flintlock he invented had a frizzen (striker) and when the trigger was pulled, a spring action caused the frizzen to strike the flint, producing sparks. So not only could it work in spite of bad weather, but also shoot faster and more accurately.

火枪

Musket

20 世纪　云南　长 127 厘米　宽 11 厘米　高 7 厘米　木、铁质

The 1900s, wood and iron, 127 cm × 11 cm × 7 cm, Yunnan

火枪
Musket

20 世纪　云南　长 154.5 厘米　宽 11 厘米　高 13 厘米　木、铁质
The 1900s, wood and iron, 154.5 cm × 11 cm × 13 cm, Yunnan

火枪
Musket

20 世纪　云南　长 115.4 厘米　宽 3 厘米　高 16 厘米　木、铁质
The 1900s, wood and iron, 115.4 cm × 3 cm × 16 cm, Yunnan

火枪
Musket

20 世纪　云南　长 133 厘米　宽 6.5 厘米　高 12 厘米　木、铁质
The 1900s, wood and iron, 133 cm × 6.5 cm × 12 cm, Yunnan

火枪
Musket

藏族　20 世纪　云南　长 122 厘米　宽 6 厘米　高 11 厘米　木、铁质
The 1900s, wood and iron, 122 cm × 6 cm × 11 cm, Tibetan, Yunnan

火枪
Musket

藏族　20 世纪　云南　长 63 厘米　宽 17 厘米　高 6 厘米　木、铁质
The 1900s, wood and iron, 63 cm × 17 cm × 6 cm, Tibetan, Yunnan

3. 火药筒袋　Gunpowder Cartridges and Bags

火药是火枪的弹药，为易燃物，保管不当会有危险。因潮湿的火药不易点燃，会导致在关键的时候使用不了火枪，所以人们用坚硬而又防潮的原皮缝制火药筒袋，还会用动物骨和角等密封性好的材料来加工制作火药筒袋。

Gunpowder for the musket was flammable and would be dangerous if not in proper storage. On the other hand, the damp powder could not be ignited, making the musket impossible to work at the critical moment, so a gunpowder cartridge or bag was made of hard and dampness-proof hides or materials with a good sealing performance like animal bones and horns.

刻花大牛角火药筒
Big Ox Horn Cartridge with Carved Pattern

藏族　20 世纪　云南　长 43 厘米　宽 18 厘米　高 15 厘米　牛角、银质
The 1900s, ox horn and silver, 43 cm × 18 cm × 15 cm, Tibetan, Yunnan

大头顶端中心雕刻八瓣莲花纹，四周有缠枝纹，中间有缠枝纹包银装饰。小头处有环形纽的金属盖子，下面有木塞，可打开装入火药。首尾之间有绳连接，方便携带。

扁口牛角火药筒
Ox Horn Cartridge with Oblate Opening

藏族　20世纪　云南　长26厘米　宽8厘米　高9厘米　牛角、银质
The 1900s, ox horn and silver, 26 cm × 8 cm × 9 cm, Tibetan, Yunnan

火药筒开口处部分包银装饰。从扁口处装入火药，盖已丢失。

带盖牛角火药筒

Ox Horn Cartridge with Cover

藏族　20 世纪　云南　长 18 厘米　宽 8 厘米　高 7 厘米　牛角、木质

The 1900s, ox horn and wood, 18 cm × 8 cm × 7 cm, Tibetan, Yunnan

由两个小牛角组成，一个带盖，另一个外接皮囊和木塞，装入火药后可用木塞堵上。两个牛角之间有绳相连，方便携带。

皮火药袋
Leather Gunpowder Bag

藏族　20 世纪　云南　长 12.5 厘米　宽 8 厘米　高 20 厘米　皮质
The 1900s, leather, 12.5 cm × 8 cm × 20 cm, Tibetan, Yunnan

水壶状，腹鼓，小口上塞有玉米芯做成的盖子，两耳有穿孔，方便系绳携带。

皮火药袋
Leather Gunpowder Bag

藏族　20 世纪　云南　长 8 厘米　宽 5 厘米　高 11 厘米　皮质
The 1900s, leather, 8 cm × 5 cm × 11 cm, Tibetan, Yunnan

水壶状，小口上有带孔的皮环帮助束口，腹鼓，两耳有穿孔，方便系绳携带。

火药袋挂饰

Pendent for Gunpowder Bag

藏族　20 世纪　云南　长 30 厘米　宽 6 厘米　高 25 厘米　牛角、皮、骨质

The 1900s, ox horn, leather and bones, 30 cm × 6 cm × 25 cm, Tibetan, Yunnan

由牛角、皮、骨等多种材质的火药筒和挂件组成。大小不一，形状各异，由皮绳串联在一起，便于携带。

火药袋挂饰

Pendent for Gunpowder Bag

藏族　20 世纪　云南　长 28 厘米　宽 7 厘米　高 32 厘米　皮质

The 1900s, leather, 28 cm × 7 cm × 32 cm, Tibetan, Yunnan

用皮绳将 3 个大小不一、形状各异的皮火药袋串联组成，方便携带。

火药袋挂饰

Pendent for Gunpowder Bag

藏族 20 世纪 云南 长 33 厘米 宽 7 厘米 高 24 厘米 皮、骨质

The 1900s, leather and bones, 33 cm × 7 cm × 24 cm, Tibetan, Yunnan

用皮绳将 3 个形状不同的皮火药袋和 2 个骨质火药筒串联而成。其中最大的一个皮火药袋呈心形，上接皮囊和木塞。

火药袋挂饰

Pendent for Gunpowder Bag

藏族　20 世纪　云南　长 36 厘米　宽 4 厘米　高 26 厘米　皮、骨、铁质

The 1900s, leather, bones and iron, 36 cm × 4 cm × 26 cm, Tibetan, Yunnan

由 6 件大小、形状各异的火药袋和挂件串联而成。其中最大的一个为皮质水壶状火药袋。

4. 其他护身工具　Other Tools for Self-protection

茶马古道上的防身工具，除了刀、枪，火药外，馆藏的还有大刀、叉、矛等防身工具。其中铁叉除了防身外，还有别的作用，如马帮在野外宿营时，钉下几个铁叉，在铁叉上吊起锅就能生火做饭。

In addition to the knives, muskets and gunpowder, the museum collection includes such tools for self-protection as machetes, tridents, spears. Especially the iron tridents also worked in other ways, for example, when camping out, members of the caravan put a few tridents slant in the ground, had a pot suspended from the crossing part of the tridents' handles and made a fire to cook.

直柄铁大刀
Iron Machete with Straight Handle

20 世纪　云南　长 191 厘米　宽 14 厘米　高 4 厘米　铁、木质
The 1900s, iron and wood, 191 cm × 14 cm × 4 cm, Yunnan

铁的短直柄上接长大刀，下接木质的长柄。

直柄月牙铁叉

Crescent Iron Fork with Straight Handle

20 世纪　云南　长 156 厘米　宽 27.2 厘米　高 3 厘米　铁、木质

The 1900s, iron and wood, 156 cm × 27.2 cm × 3 cm, Yunnan

铁的短柄上接月牙形的铁叉，下接木质的长柄。

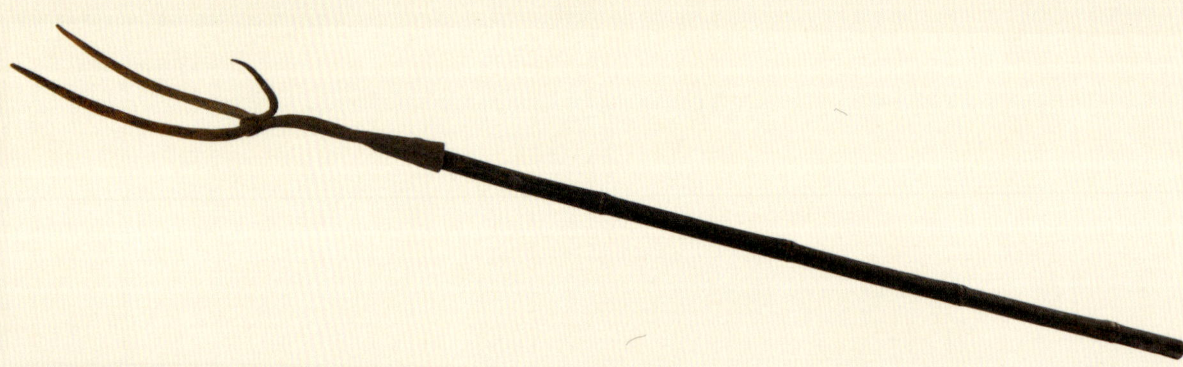

直柄铁三叉

Iron Trident with Straight Handle

20 世纪　云南　长 152 厘米　宽 20 厘米　高 9 厘米　铁、竹质

The 1900s, iron and bamboo, 152 cm × 20 cm × 9 cm, Yunnan

短的铁柄上接铁质三叉，两边的长叉大致相同，中间的短叉凸起呈倒钩状，下接竹质长柄。

直柄铁三叉

Iron Trident with Straight Handle

20 世纪　云南　长 155.3 厘米　宽 35 厘米　高 3.5 厘米　铁、木质

The 1900s, iron and wood, 155.3 cm × 35 cm × 3.5 cm, Yunnan

铁柄贯穿成为居中的一叉，两旁等长的两叉从它中间穿孔连接固定，下接木质长柄。

直柄铁三叉

Iron Trident with Straight Handle

20 世纪　云南　长 164.3 厘米　宽 29 厘米　高 3 厘米　铁、竹质

The 1900s, iron and bamboo, 164.3 cm × 29 cm × 3 cm, Yunnan

铁柄贯穿成为居中的一叉，叉尖似短剑状，其底部有孔，月牙形两叉从孔中穿过固定，下接竹质长柄。

直柄铁矛
Iron Spear with Straight Handle

20 世纪　云南　长 130 厘米　宽 5.5 厘米　高 3 厘米　铁、木质
The 1900s, iron and wood, 130 cm × 5.5 cm × 3 cm, Yunnan

短铁柄上接短剑状矛头，下接木质的长柄。矛头的底端还有两个弯曲的倒钩刺。

直柄铁矛
Iron Spear with Straight Handle

20 世纪　云南　长 145 厘米　宽 5.5 厘米　高 3.5 厘米　铁、木质
The 1900s, iron and wood, 145 cm × 5.5 cm × 3.5 cm, Yunnan

短铁柄上接短剑状矛头，中间有一个圆箍状的铁件，铁柄下接木质的长柄。

五、马帮常用乐器 The Caravan's Common Musical Instruments

马帮一路风餐露宿，非常辛苦，他们的身体和精神都需要放松。音乐可以抚慰他们疲惫的身心，因此演奏乐器就成了他们表达情感和转换心情最好的方式。茶马古道上有句俗语："赶马路上有唱不完的调子。"三弦、二胡、葫芦笙、芦笙等是他们唱山歌、吟小调时常用的伴奏乐器。而马帮最常用的铜锣，其主要作用则是开道示警。有时狭窄的古道只能容一匹马通过，这时马帮要及时敲锣，用铜锣声告知渐渐靠近的路人，这里有一队马队走来，只有相互谦让，才能平安。后来慢慢形成了不成文的规矩，请人让路就敲"咚……咚……咚……"，有事告急就连续急促地敲"咚咚咚"。藏族马帮还有一种吹奏乐器"岗洞"，藏语称扎令，译为腿号，原型是胫骨号，后来多用金属制成。

After an arduous journey, the caravan needed to unwind, and music was able to soothe their tired body and mind. Therefore, playing musical instruments became the best way to express feelings and elevate the spirit. As a saying goes there, "And all it's hill songs unsung on the road". Sanxian (a three-stringed Chinese lute), Chinese fiddle (a two-stringed bowed instrument), Hulusheng, lusheng (a reed-pipe wind instrument), were common accompanying instruments when they sang hill songs or chanted ditties. Yet Chinese gongs were the most commonly used to give a warning to make way. When some narrow path could allow only a single horse to pass through, they needed to beat a gong in time informing the approaching traveler of the caravan coming along and warning that safety would be guaranteed only if they yielded to each other. It gradually became unwritten rules that when the gong sounded "Tong—tong—tong—, it meant asking the others to yield, and when sounded "Tong tong tong", it signaled urgency. The Tibetan caravan also used a wind instrument called "Gangdong", or "Zhaling" in Tibetan, meant leg horn, which was originally made of shinbone but later mostly made of metal.

大三弦
Big Sanxian

20 世纪　云南　长 24.3 厘米　宽 8 厘米　高 103 厘米　木、蟒皮质
The 1900s, wood and boa skin, 24.3 cm × 8 cm × 103 cm, Yunnan

三弦，又称“弦子”，弦鸣乐器。主要由琴头、琴轴、琴杆和琴鼓（音箱）四部分组成。此琴头呈四方形，琴轴悬挂着弹拨用的骨质指甲，琴鼓蟒皮已损，琴弦遗失，琴杆上系红绳便于携带。在茶马古道沿途，三弦是流传很广的乐器，有大小三弦之分。三弦的音量较大，琴声清脆，变化多样，既可以独奏，又可以合奏，是马帮途中弹唱山歌调子伴奏常用的乐器之一。

二胡

Chinese Fiddle

20 世纪　云南　长 13 厘米　宽 8.4 厘米　高 75 厘米　木、皮质

The 1900s, wood and skin, 13 cm × 8.4 cm × 75 cm, Yunnan

二胡，又名“胡琴”，拉弦乐器。一般的二胡琴头常雕刻成龙首或呈弯月形。此琴头则为尖头，方便插入驮包随身携带。琴轴上端装两个弦轴，下端插入琴筒，弓弦已损坏断裂，琴筒一侧系有红绳便于固定。二胡的声音低沉哀怨，能酣畅淋漓地表达赶马人对家人和故乡的思念之情。

月琴
Gekkin

彝族　20 世纪　云南　长 36.5 厘米　宽 6.5 厘米　高 63 厘米　木质
The 1900s, wood, 36.5 cm × 6.5 cm × 63 cm, Yi, Yunnan

月琴，又称“四弦”，弦鸣乐器。此琴头已损坏，琴轴余两根，琴颈短小，琴身为音箱，外形较大呈满圆形，中间雕刻中国传统的二龙戏珠图案，有庆丰年、祈吉祥之寓意，边缘有一圈寓意“富贵不断头”的回纹。这些图案和纹饰是茶马古道上民族融合的具体呈现。月琴 200 年前已流行于西南彝族聚居区。云南巍山文昌宫桥墩壁画《彝族踏歌图》（17 世纪）中就绘有弹月琴的舞者。月琴音量较小，音色清脆柔和，非常适合赶马人抒情性的说唱伴奏。

葫芦笙
Hulusheng

20 世纪 云南 长 19.5 厘米 宽 8 厘米 高 51 厘米 葫芦、竹质
The 1900s, gourd and bamboo, 19.5 cm × 8 cm × 51 cm, Yunnan

葫芦笙，古称“瓢笙”，为吹奏乐器，流行于滇、黔、川、桂等地。葫芦为笙斗，细端穿孔接一长管为吹口，笙管由黄枯竹制成，一般四至八管不等，长短不一，环列并微穿葫芦腹部以蜡固定，每管靠近葫芦处开一按音孔。葫芦笙吹奏简单，小巧轻便，适宜马帮长途携带。

芦笙
Lusheng

苗族 20 世纪 云南 长 76 厘米 宽 6.5 厘米 高 73.5 厘米 木、竹质
The 1900s, wood and bamboo, 76 cm × 6.5 cm × 73.5 cm, Miao, Yunnan

芦笙，古称“卢沙”，现称“九点”，为吹奏乐器。流行于黔、桂、滇、湘、川等地，由笙斗、笙管、簧片和共鸣筒组成。笙斗用木制成，细端插一竹管吹嘴，中间掏空后装入笙管后再用胶粘合，笙管用细长的竹子制成。笙管一般为六管，也有四管或八管的。此六管芦笙有两管已遗失，只余穿孔。芦笙轻便易携带，往驮包里一插就可上路。芦笙的音色欢快明亮，让人一听就心情愉悦，因此受到马帮人的青睐。

铜锣

Gong

20 世纪　云南　直径 50 厘米　高 1 厘米　铜质

The 1900s, copper, 50 cm in diameter and 1 cm in height, Yunnan

铜锣又称“铓锣”。圆形，中间有一个半圆形凸起，凸起的四周有花瓣状金光闪闪的太阳纹饰。铜锣边缘有数道圆圈纹，侧面有穿孔，系红绳便于手提。铓锣声声，曾给寂静的山林增添了几许生气。

铜锣
Gong

20 世纪　云南　直径 30 厘米　高 9 厘米　铜质
The 1900s, copper, 30 cm in diameter and 9 cm in height, Yunnan

表面平素无纹，中间有一个半圆形凸起，边缘有磨损。

岗洞
Gangdong

藏族 20 世纪 云南 长 35 厘米 宽 8 厘米 高 4 厘米 铜质
The 1900s, copper, 35 cm × 8 cm × 4 cm, Tibetan, Yunnan

岗洞又称“岗林”，为吹奏乐器。由从细到粗的三节铜管组成，最后一节的末端上雕刻两个眼睛和一个鼻子，底部露出的部分像其张大的嘴，声音就从这神秘的嘴中发出来。岗洞无固定音高，音色粗犷，发呜呜声，其乐有招神之意。

六、马帮契约文书 Contractual Documents of Caravans

在征集马帮文物时，还征集到了一批清代、民国时期的地方契约文书。这些文书记录了300余年间滇西民众的日常活动，既涉及土地的流动、家业的荣枯，也包含村族内的守望相助、邻里间的纷争纠葛，基本勾勒出那个时代滇西民众生活的纷繁世相，是生动鲜活的民族生产与生活的记录，是支撑区域社会史研究的重要史料，有很高的学术研究价值，体现了多元一体的大一统国家制度与文化认同，尤其是对研究中华各民族交往、交流、交融的历史具有重要的意义。

从目前整理出的866件文书中，我们发现一件和马帮相关的契约文书。此文书详细记录了1803年一个叫杨汝柽的人将一块秧田卖给大锅头（马帮首领）李玉瑞一事，从侧面反映出当时马帮的兴盛和马锅头的富有。

Along with the caravan's artifacts, a batch of local contractual documents in the Qing dynasty and the period of Republic of China have been collected. They reveal the daily activities of western Yunnan people within 300 years, covering not only transfer of land rights and vicissitude of family property but also mutual help and protection in a hamlet and disputation and entanglement between neighbors, which basically give a complicated picture of western Yunnan people's life in the times and are the vivid records of the different ethnic peoples' production and living. What's more, these documents are the important historical materials with highly academic value for the study of the regional social history and show a national unified system with diversity and cultural identity, which are significant to the study of the history of contact, interaction and blending between various Chinese peoples.

Among the collated 866 documents, an agreement is associated with the caravan. It details a person named Yang Rucheng selling a rice paddy to Li Yurui, a Maguotou (head of a caravan), reflecting the prosperity of the caravan and the wealth of Maguotou at that time.

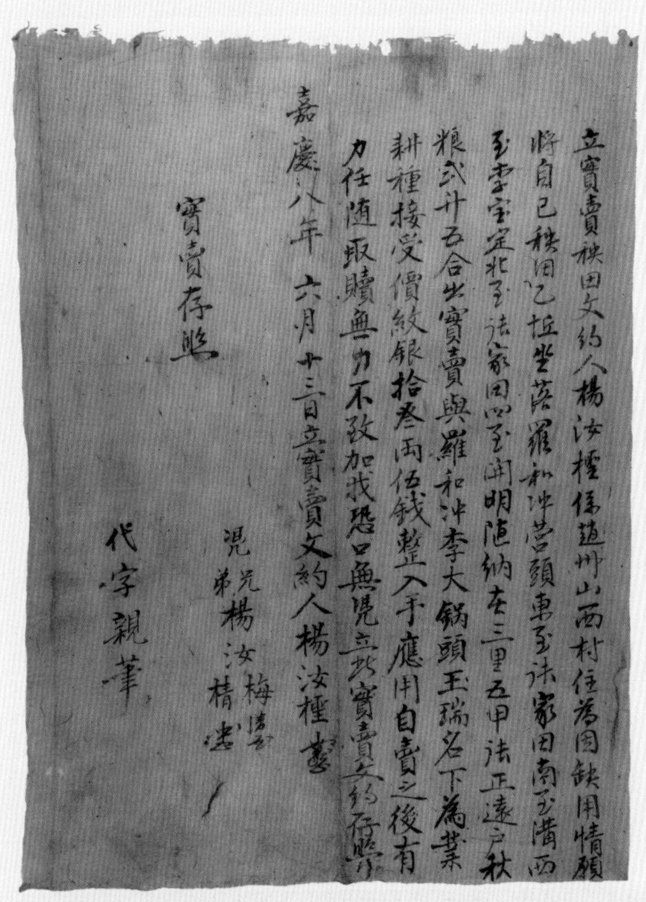
立實賣秧田文約人楊汝樫係趙州山西村住為因缺用情願
將自己秧田一坵坐落羅和沖營頭東至張家田南至溝西
至李宝定北至張家田四至開明隨納庄三里五甲張正遠戶秋
糧貳升五合出實賣與羅和沖李大鍋頭玉瑞名下為業
耕種接受價紋銀拾叁兩伍錢整入手應用自賣之後有
力任隨取贖無力不致加找恐口無憑立此實賣文約存照
嘉慶八年六月十三日立實賣文約人楊汝樫
憑兄楊汝梅
弟楊汝精
實賣存照
代字親筆

嘉庆八年六月十三日杨汝柽立实卖秧田文约

A Contract Signed by Yang Rucheng to Sell His Rice Paddy on June 13, 1803

1803 年 〔清〕大理府赵州（今大理白族自治州大理市凤仪镇） 纵 39 厘米 横 27.7 厘米

1803, 39 cm × 27.7 cm, Zhaozhou, Dali Prefecture,Qing dynasty (now Fengyi Village, Dali, Dali Bai Autonomous Prefecture)

实录文如下：

立实卖秧田文约人杨汝柽系赵州山西村住为因缺用情愿
将自己秧田一坵坐落罗和冲营头东至张家田南至沟西
至李宝定北至张家田四至开明随纳庄三里五甲张正远户秋
粮贰升五合出实卖与罗和冲李大锅头玉瑞名下为业
耕种接受价纹银十三两五钱整入手应用自卖之后有
力任随取赎无力不致加找恐口无凭立此实卖文约存照
嘉庆八年六月十三日立实卖文约人杨汝柽（押）
凭兄杨汝梅
凭弟杨汝精
实卖存照
代字亲笔

第三单元 巍山——马帮老家

Part Ⅲ Weishan—the Hometown of Caravans

巍山北与大理市相连，东经过云南驿通往昆明，南经过景东通往普洱，西经过永平通往缅甸。过去数百年，这里成了滇西运输的重要枢纽和茶马古道必经之地。同时它也是“三进三出”茶文化传播的中枢。“三进”的第一条是从勐海、普洱、景东进入蒙化（巍山）；第二条是从耿马、双江、临沧、云县进入；第三条是从凤庆、茶房寺进入。“三出”的第一条是从隆庆关过弥渡、昆明、成都、西安至北京；第二条是从瓦房哨、大理、香格里拉、拉萨出尼泊尔、印度；第三条是从永平、保山、芒市至瑞丽出缅甸。因此，巍山在清代被御封为“文献名邦”，1994 年被列为国家级历史文化名城，2007 年被云南省列为茶马古道重镇并立有石碑。

Weishan bordering Dali in the north, leading to Kunming by way of Yunnanyi in the east, through Jingdong to Pu'er in the south, and through Yongping to Myanmar in the west. Over past several hundred years, it has been a transportation center in western Yunnan and a place whoever traveled along the Ancient Tea-Horse Road had to pass through. At the same time, it is also the central hub for the dissemination of “three in and three out” tea culture. The “three-in” refers to the three ways into Weishan: way one starting from Menghai, Pu'er and Jingdong into Menghua(Weishan); way two from Gengma, Shuangjiang, Lincang and Yunxian; and way three from Fengqing and Chafangsi. The “three-out” means the three ways out of Menghua: way one starting from Longqing pass through Midu, Kunming, Chengdu and Xi'an to Beijing; way two from Wafangshao, Dali, Shangri-La and Lhasa to Nepal and India; way three from Yongping, Baoshan, Mangshi and Ruili to Myanmar. Therefore, Weishan was granted the title of “Prestigious Town of Documents” by the imperial court in the Qing dynasty, listed as a national town of history and culture in 1994, and designated the hub on the Ancient Tea-Horse Road by Yunnan Government and to which a monument was erected in 2007.

巍山自古以来几乎户户养马，直至今日巍山有些地方仍保留马市。因此巍山马帮众多，被称为“马帮的老家”。据有关资料统计，民国年间，全县有驮马 7800 匹；1949 年，全县有马帮 204 支、驮马 7784 匹；1954 年，全县有马帮 344 支、驮马 9593 匹；1959 年，以公社为单位组织起 11 支马帮运输大队，有驮马 4502 匹。为适应马帮的需求，巍山古城内许多马具店便应运而生，出售马的全部行头，同时还有很多马掌铺，生产各种规格的马掌和马钉。抗日战争时期，云南与东南亚陆路之间的交通运输是抗战生命线，以东莲花 7 支大马帮为首的巍山回族马帮，在全长 600 多公里的滇缅干线上，组织了 700 多匹骡马抢运物资，为抗战胜利作出了重要

巍山古城楼

茶马古道重镇蒙化碑

鸟道雄关

巍山鸟道雄关附近茶马古道上的马蹄窝

贡献。

巍山除了马帮老家外，还有多张名片，如南诏古都、彝祖故里、道教圣地、鸟道雄关、红河之源、民间扎染艺术之乡等。其中巍山隆庆关的鸟道雄关，处于西南丝绸古道人马驿道的重要通口，至今那里还遗留着深深的马蹄印，仿佛在诉说着当年的故事。

巍山多民族聚居，境内有 23 个民族，其中汉、彝、回、白、苗、傈僳为世居民族。来来往往的马帮促进了巍山经济和文化的繁荣发展。从巍山马家大院，以及工艺品、药材等茶马互市的交易物中，我们可以一窥当时马帮老家的盛况。

巍山茶马古道第一桥——永济桥（明代万历元年，即公元 1573 年始建）

茶房寺

茶房寺附近的古道

Since ancient times almost every household in Weishan raised horses, and even today horse markets remain in parts of Weishan. Therefore, there were a lot of caravans and it was called "the Hometown of Caravans". According to relevant statistical data, there were 7,800 pack horses in the period of the Republic of China; 204 caravans and 7,784 pack horses in 1949; 344 caravans and 9,593 pack horses in 1954; communes, as the basic units of rural areas, organized 11 big caravans with 4,502 pack horses in 1959. To meet caravans' needs, many harness shops appeared in the old town of Weishan, selling all the saddlery, meanwhile, a lot of farrieries making horseshoes of various sizes and horseshoe nails. During the Chinese People's War of Resistance against Japanese Aggression, the land transportation between Yunnan and Southeast Asia was a lifeline for the war, and the Hui caravan group in Weishan, consisting chiefly of Donglianhua's seven caravans, mobilized over 700 pack animals to do the emergency transportation of goods along the Yunnan-Myanmar route with a total length of more than 600 km, making an important contribution to the victory of the war.

Aside from the hometown of caravans, Weishan is known as the ancient capital of Nanzhao, the native place of the Yi people's ancestor, the holy land of Taoism, the Hard Pass for the Bird, the Source of Red River, and the town of tie-dyeing techniques. Especially the Hard Pass for the Bird at Longqing Pass, Weishan lies at the key pass of the ancient Silk Road in Southern China, where clear prints of horse's hoofs remain, as if telling what happened there.

Weishan is a multi-ethnic place, in which Han, Yi, Hui, Bai, Miao, and Lishu of the 23 ethnic groups are native peoples. Coming and going caravans contributed to the prosperity and development of economy and culture in Weishan. From the Ma's Mansion in Weishan, and from what was transacted in the Tea for Horse Market like handicrafts and medicinal herbs, we can get a glimpse into the boom of the hometown of caravans.

一、马家大院 Ma's Mansion

马家大院为巍山东莲花村回族马锅头于 1941 年建成的古建筑群。马家大院多采用“六合同春”布局，角楼林立，重门深院，“三坊一照壁”“四合五天井”“走马转阁楼”等建筑工艺十分精湛。无论是照壁还是雕花，都体现着各民族文化的和谐并存、水乳交融。其走廊设计也十分人性化，无论刮风下雨，都不用打伞戴帽，能从容进入任何一个房间，走廊的宽度是依照马身的宽度修建的，云南马在走廊里能够正常通行。

马帮传奇马锅头马如骥的旧居是马家大院古建筑群当中的典范，特色是“一碉两院三门四阁五堂六天井”。二楼藻井有彩绘《三文笔》《鸡足山》《上海街景》。特别是彩绘《上海街景》，被专家视为不可多得的珍贵资料，它再现了当年十里洋场上海滩的风华。马如骥大院旁边建立了一座东莲花村马帮文化博物馆，以马如骥为代表的巍山马帮的事迹为后人所缅怀和颂扬。

马家大院里的照壁

马如骥大院

马如骥大院

马家大院

东莲花村马帮文化博物馆

东莲花村马帮文化博物馆展品

It is an old architectural complex built in 1941 by the Hui maguotou in Donglianhua Hemlet, Weisan County. It mostly laid out in the form of "the six compounds in one complex", with corner towers and connecting courtyards; the compound with three houses and a screen wall, the compound with four multi-storied buildings, one main courtyard and four side yards and the covered corridor connecting the different buildings were exquisitely designed and made. The screen wall or carved patterns shows the co-existence and blending of various ethnic cultures. Designed in the user friendly way, the covered corridor can protect one from rain or wind so that one can go unhurriedly into any room without using an umbrella or wearing a cap. And the width of the corridor was designed according to the horse, so the Yunan pony can pass through easily.

The legendary maguotou Ma Ruji's former residence is the typical example of the Ma's Mansion, characterized by "one watchtower, two courtyards, three gates, four multi-storied buildings, five principal rooms and six side yards". On the ceilings of the second floor go with color paintings of "Sanwenbi Village", "Jizu Mount" and "Shanghai Streetscapes". Particularly the last, valued highly as rare historic records by experts, reveals the then flourishing Bund in Shanghai. Donglianhua Museum of Caravan Culture stands next to Ma's Mansion, so the caravan's stories represented by Ma Ruji will be remembered and extolled.

二、茶马互市中的其他交易物 Other Transactions in the Tea for Horse Market

我国唐代就实行了专门的“茶马互市”，制定了茶叶贸易的政策并实行茶税，它是中原汉族与周边少数民族经济往来的主要形式。但随着不同时代的发展，茶马互市逐渐成了茶叶和土特产之间的贸易。明清以后从内地输入青藏高原最主要的物品就是茶叶、丝绸、布匹、纸张、金属制品、玻璃制品、玉石、香料、工艺品、日用品、佛教用品等。青藏高原向内地输出的物品以畜牧产品和土特产为主，如马、绵羊、牦牛尾、天然矿物、盐、沙金、药材、宝石以及金银器、毛纺织品等。

马帮走到哪里，哪里就成为一个集市。在马店集中的巍山，就形成了一个大集市。那时候从巍山出发或者到巍山来的马帮，都装满了各地的特产，在巍山交易后，又驮往各地销售。特别是春茶前后，经常有上万匹骡马经过，使巍山成为一座马帮的城市，一个商品交易非常活跃的城市。据说最热闹的时候，一天大约有 4000 人在此交易。现今我们可以从以下保存下来的工艺品和药材中看到一些当时商品交易的情况。

The Tea for Horse Market started in the Tang dynasty when a tea trade policy was made and tax was levied on tea, which was the main form of economic ties between the Han people in the Central Plains and the ethnic groups around. But with the development of the times, it evolved into a tea for local specialties market. After the Ming and Qing dynasties, what was mainly brought into Tibet included tea, silk, fabrics, paper, metalwork, glassware, jade, spices, craftwork, daily necessities, Buddhism items, etc. What was brought out were livestock products and local specialties, like horses, sheep, yak tail, natural minerals, salt, alluvial gold, medicinal herbs, precious stones, gold and silver wares, wool fabrics, and so forth.

Wherever caravans went, a market would appear. A big market came into existence in Weishan where there were a lot of caravans. At that time, all caravans coming into Weishan with full loads of specialties from different places used to transact there and then carry what they bought to other areas for sale. Especially around the time when spring tea was in season, tens of thousands of pack animals passed through, making Weishan a town of caravans and an active market. It is said that when it was the busiest, about 4,000 people transacted there a day. Now we can see how exchanges of goods took place from the following handicrafts and medicinal herbs that survive.

1. 工艺品 Craftwork

茶马古道上的交易物中，有不少体现人们精神需求和审美情趣的工艺品。馆藏的有辟邪镇宅的陶猫，怪兽驮弥勒佛香炉，树鹿雕像，佛教内容的挂像、画等。现今陶猫文化既有延续，更有创新，云南大理古城商店的陶猫文创产品随处可见。

Among the transactions, there were plenty of handicrafts embodying the then people's spiritual needs and aesthetic taste. The museum collection includes tile cat for warding off evil, incense burner of the monster carrying Maitreya, figurine of deer and tree, hanging images and paintings about Buddhism. Nowadays, the tile cat culture keeps modernizing as well as preserves its traditional features and its cultural and creative products are seen everywhere in shops of the old town in Dali, Yunnan.

镇宅陶猫

Tile Cat for Warding off Evil

20 世纪　云南　长 16 厘米　宽 10 厘米　高 21 厘米　陶质
The 1900s, pottery, 16 cm × 10 cm × 21 cm, Yunnan

仰天大张的盘状嘴，露出牙和舌头，鼻子、眼睛和尖尖的耳朵长在头顶，背上还刻有一对八卦阴阳鱼图案。陶猫为云南特有的看家护宅、驱邪纳福的镇宅神兽。按当地民俗，房屋建好后通常都要请（买）一个陶猫，请“经公”（音）念经、开光后，安放在屋脊正中，以此来辟邪、镇宅、保平安。

怪兽驮弥勒佛陶香炉

Pottery Incense Burner of the Monster Carrying Maitreya

20 世纪　云南　长 22 厘米　宽 19 厘米　高 18 厘米　陶质

The 1900s, pottery, 22 cm × 19 cm × 18 cm, Yunnan

怪兽大嘴张开，露出两颗獠牙，眼睛外鼓，孔状鼻，两耳竖起，前面两足下蹲，背上有许多涡旋纹饰。驮着的弥勒佛像，笑容可掬，手捧法器。佛像可以和底座分开，下面中空，可贮存香灰，背后有 3 个孔用来插香。

树鹿木雕像

Wooden Figurine of Deer and Tree

20 世纪　云南　长 18.5 厘米　宽 10 厘米　高 20.5 厘米　木质
The 1900s, wood, 18.5 cm × 10 cm × 20.5 cm, Yunnan

用木头雕刻而成。一棵大树下，一只小鹿悠闲自得地吃草，鹿尾翘起，神态安详。在中国传统文化中，鹿和“禄”谐音，有加官进爵之寓意。

彩绘木雕佛挂像

Hanging Idol of Painted Wood Carving Buddha

藏族　20 世纪　长 22 厘米　厚 2 厘米　高 30 厘米　木质

The 1900s, wood, 22 cm × 2 cm × 30 cm, Tibetan

彩绘木雕文殊挂像

Hanging Idol of Painted Wood Carving Manjusri

藏族　20 世纪　长 56 厘米　厚 3 厘米　高 75 厘米　木质

The 1900s, wood, 56 cm × 3 cm × 75 cm, Tibetan

彩绘木雕准提佛母挂像

Hanging Idol of Painted Wood Carving Cundi

藏族 20 世纪 长 55 厘米 厚 3 厘米 高 74 厘米 木质

The 1900s, wood, 55 cm × 3 cm × 74 cm, Tibetan

彩线织上师唐卡

Colored-yarn-weaved Thang-ga of Guru

藏族　20 世纪　长 89 厘米　宽 58 厘米　布质

The 1900s, fabric, 89 cm × 58 cm, Tibetan

彩线织三世佛唐卡
Colored-yarn-weaved Thang-ga of Trikaya

藏族 20世纪 长88厘米 宽59厘米 布质
The 1900s, fabric, 88 cm × 59 cm, Tibetan

彩线织药师佛唐卡

Colored-yarn-weaved Thang-ga of Bhaisajyaguru

藏族　20 世纪　长 88 厘米　宽 58 厘米　布质

The 1900s, fabric, 88 cm × 58 cm, Tibetan

彩线织莲花生唐卡

Colored-yarn-weaved Thang-ga of Padmasambhava

藏族 20世纪 长89厘米 宽58.3厘米 布质

The 1900s, fabric, 89 cm × 58.3 cm, Tibetan

2. 药材 Medicinal Herbs

在茶马古道上，药材是最主要的交换和贸易物品，有鹿茸、虫草、贝母、黄连、牛黄、虎骨、香菌、藏红花等。现馆藏遗存下来的药材有藏羚羊角、鬣羚角、树舌灵芝等。

In the Ancient Tea-Horse Road, medicinal herbs were one of the major transactions, such as pilose antler, Chinese caterpillar fungus, fritillaria, Chinese goldthread, cow bezoar, tiger bone, shiitake, saffron crocus, etc. Now the collection includes chiru horn, mainland serow horn, ganoderma applanatum, and so on.

树舌灵芝
Ganoderma Applanatum

20 世纪　云南　长 56 厘米　宽 37 厘米　高 37.5 厘米　木栓质
The 1900s, suberin, 56 cm × 37 cm × 37.5 cm, Yunnan

树舌灵芝又称树舌扁灵芝，无柄，菌盖半圆形。树舌，意为树长的舌头，多长在树干上。树舌灵芝广泛分布于我国的大江南北，种类繁多，状似灵芝，却没有灵芝那样长的柄，可药用。

后　记

滇藏茶马古道是茶马古道中重要的主干道之一，它不仅是一条商贸通道，更是贯穿着历史文化的精神载体。中国各民族之间的交往、交流、交融，除了文字记载的“大事”外，更多地体现在像茶叶、药材、土特产等这样不起眼但又与普通百姓日常生活息息相关的具体物资的交流之中。以茶叶等商品的互通有无为纽带，各民族相互交往、相互信赖、守望相助，密切了命运共同体的历史联系和民间情义。当今为成就世界各国人民共同美好未来的“一带一路”，可以说是茶马古道精神在历史新阶段的弘扬传播和生动再现。为了更好地了解和理解，进而挖掘和利用好馆藏茶马古道历史文化遗产的价值，我们从云南省巍山县这个昔日滇藏线马帮文化重镇征集而来的马帮文物和巍山藏品中选出 260 余件纳入本书。这些展示各民族交往、交流、交融密切关系的珍贵文物鲜活展现在我们面前，让我们感动，使我们更加珍惜今天伟大祖国交通畅达、物资丰裕、民族团结、人民幸福、社会和谐的欣欣向荣局面。

在编撰过程中，我们查阅和参照了大量的文献资料，并对滇藏茶马古道云南沿线中的景洪、勐海、澜沧、普洱、镇沅、巍山、大理、剑川、香格里拉、德钦等十多个县市进行了考察和调研，通过探寻古道、野生千年古茶树，参观茶厂和当地的博物馆，寻访马帮后人和马具制作人，实地探寻马店遗址等方式来进行研究和考证，力求做到尊重历史，反映事实。实地亲身走过这条道路，我们才领略到滇藏茶马古道的险峻，才真正体会到当年的马帮所经受的艰难困苦，也才深刻地感受到茶马古道所包容的人文精神的博大精深。本书编撰后期，我们聘请了故宫博物院陶瓷专家王光尧先生、巍山文史专家范建伟先生和西藏文化博物馆研究部主任当增扎西先生审阅了相关内容。在此，要特别感谢范建伟先生的鼎力支持，他无偿地提供了马帮的照片，并给予了宝贵的意见和建议，使我们受益匪浅。由于时间仓促，藏品的原始资料多有空缺，还有许多问题仍需要我们进一步研究和探讨。本书如有不当之处，恳请大家批评指正。

编　者

2023 年 6 月

Afterword

The Yunnan-Tibet route was one of the key routes of the Ancient Tea-Horse Road, not only a commerce and trade passage, but a spiritual carrier that runs through history and culture. The contact, interaction and blending between the ethnic groups in China was, aside from in the "events" recorded in words, more reflected in the physical exchange of goods like tea, medicinal herbs, local specialties that were common but closely related to the ordinary people's daily life. With exchanges of needed goods like tea as ties of folk friendship, the mutual interaction, mutual trust and mutual help among the various peoples has laid a historical foundation for the sense of community for the Chinese nation. Today, the "Belt and Road" initiative to achieve a better shared future for the whole world may be regarded as the continuation, dissemination and vivid recreation of the "Ancient Tea-Horse Road" spirit in the new times. To better know and understand and then fully tap the cultural heritage from the Ancient Tea-Horse Road in the museum collection, we have selected over 260 pieces in the collection from Weishan, Yunnan, a hub of caravans on the Yunnan-Tibet route in the past, and in the Weishan collection, and included them in this book. Moved at the rare physical objects suggesting the close relationship between various ethnic groups, we will even more cherish our booming situation in which there are great facilities of communication, material wealth, ethnic unity, the people's sense of happiness and social harmony.

In the process of compiling, we have referred to a large amount of literature and made on-the-spot investigation in over 10 counties and cities along the Yunnan leg of the Yunnan-Tibet route such as Jinghong, Weishan and Deqin, exploring the ancient paths, observing thousand-year-old wild tea trees, visiting the tea factories and local museums, searching and interviewing the descendants of the caravans and the harness-makers, studying and verifying the sites of the caravansaries, so as to strive to respect history and give an accurate picture. Travelling along the road personally, we know its steepness, truly understand the difficulties and hardships the caravans experienced and deeply feel the broadness and profoundness of the humanistic spirit the Ancient Tea-Horse Road embodies. At the later stage of compiling the book, Mr. Wang Guangyao, an expert in ceramics in the Palace Museum, Mr. Fan Jianwei, an expert on literature and history in Weishan, and Mr. Dangzengzaxi, director of the research department of Museum of Tibetan Culture, have been invited to review the relevant parts of the book. Here special thanks go to Mr. Fan Jianwei for his great support, his free photos of caravans and his valuable criticism and advice, from which we benefit a lot. Because of time being limited and some original data about a certain object being missing, a number of questions need to be further studied and discussed. It would be appreciated if any criticism or suggestion could be offered.

The compiler
June, 2023